OUR MEMORIE
The history of Llanr

Pat Williams

OUR MEMORIES OF LLANRHIDIAN

The history of Llanrhidian recalled by its villagers

Compiled by Pat Williams

Published by
The Llanrhidian Local History Group

Copyright © The Llanrhidian Local History Group 2004

Published in 2004 by
The Llanrhidian Local History Group
c/o Big House, Llanrhidian
Swansea, SA3 1ER

*All rights reserved. No part of this publication may be reproduced,
stored in a retrieval system or transmitted, in any form or by any
means without the prior permission of the publisher, nor be otherwise
circulated in any form of binding or cover other than that
in which it is published and without similar condition
being imposed on the subsequent purchaser.*

A CIP catalogue record for this book is
available from the British Library.

ISBN 0-9547450-0-0

Printed and bound in Wales by
Dinefwr Press Ltd.
Rawlings Road, Llandybie
Carmarthenshire, SA18 3YD

Cover photograph:
Painting of Cross House, 1908.
Ethel Grove is milking the cow, Bertie Grove is the boy on the left,
and William Thomas is sitting on the stone outcrop.
(Painting by kind permission of Wilma Collins).

Contents

1: Schooldays in Llanrhidian 7

2: World War I 17

3: World War II 31

4: Llanrhidian at Work 70

5: Leisure Time 139

6: Llanrhidian Marsh 165

7: I Remember 171

Acknowledgements 176

MEMORIES OF LLANRHIDIAN

Llanrhidian Local History Group was formed in January 2003, so that the social history of the last century could be recorded by the villagers themselves. Here, in their own words, is their story.

1

Schooldays in Llanrhidian

The first parochial school in Llanrhidian.

Eric Morgan writes . . .
The first parochial school in Llanrhidian was in the present church hall. In the 1880s, Louisa Dunn (later Davies) of Leason Farm paid one penny a week to attend classes there. On the 5th July 1881 she sat the Third Standard Examination and passed.

Gower Church Magazine, 1908 . . .
Some people complain that they find it difficult to keep their children at school until they are 14, while there are so many desirous to employ them if they were

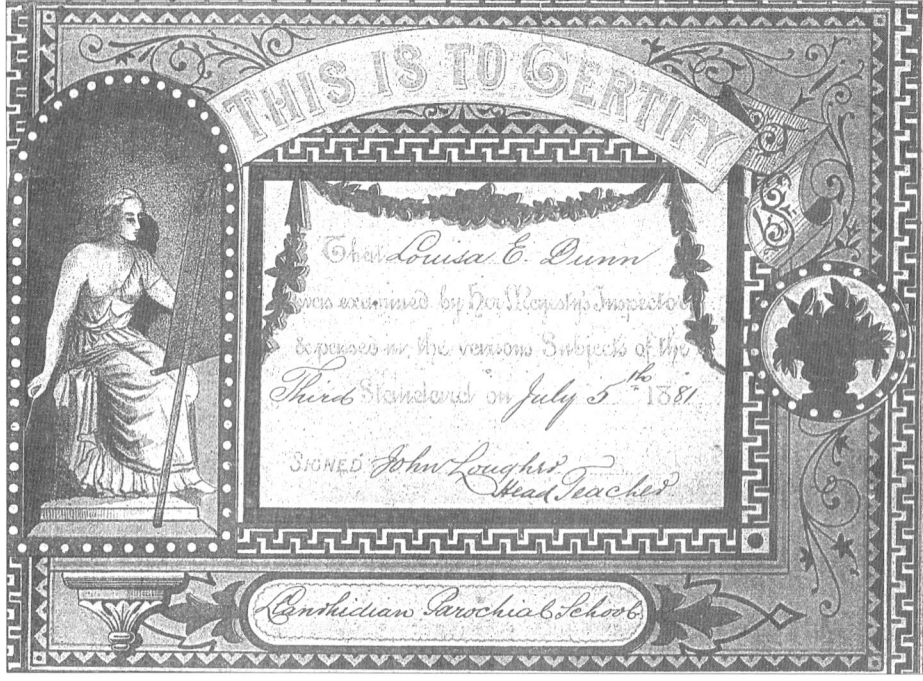

Third Standard certificate.
The headmaster of the day, Mr. M.O. Lougher, notes in his log book that the examination took place at 9 a.m. and 34 boys and 36 girls were examined. On the 7th September 1910, the new school was opened at its present premises, in a field originally owned by J. Parry Williams.

The new school, Llanrhidian.

free from school. But there is always the opportunity of getting out at an earlier age by passing the "labour" examination. This, however, is not likely to be accomplished unless the children are sent very regularly in their earlier years. Unless this is done, there is little chance of their being proficient enough to pass the examination.

Violet Davies of Leason Farm (Louisa's daughter), sat this examination and passed. She was able to leave school to look after her brothers and sisters, but always regretted that she was not able to finish her education.

Gower Church Magazine, 1908 . . .
Robson's Act – there are provisions made to enable lads to be used during the harvest operations who are not free from school. Any lad who has been regular at school, is more than eleven years old, and intends to remain in school till fourteen years of age can be employed at harvest time.

School Log Books, 1879-1936

On his first day as Master in 1879, Mr. T. J. Lewis lamented the lack of books and apparatus, and that "one third of the scholars are without slates." The log book from this date shows how the yearly farming cycle intruded into the school terms, to the increasing frustration of the Master.

8th September 1879: "very thin attendance – the lateness of the harvest may be attributable." By the 15th September, the Master decided to break up school for the remainder of the week to "allow children to assist in gathering the harvest." On the 13th April 1888, there was a "very poor school – some children kept home for potato setting." Attendance was "thin" on the 1st July 1898, because it was the day of the Swansea Wool Fair, and on the 8th July 1898, "all neighbourhood engaged in haymaking, hence the reasons for the smallness of attendance." A shooting party being engaged at Parc le Breos and Cillibion on the 18th December 1899 was the cause of "small attendance today – the bigger boys are away beating." On the 6th April 1900, the log book notes that "attendance has fallen very much this week, today especially Palm Sunday coming on, several children are away gathering flowers and doing up the graves of their departed friends." On the 23rd November 1900, "attendance has suffered considerably as several of the larger children being kept home to gather in and store the fruits of the earth, viz. potatoes, mangolds, etc."

There were other distractions apart from agriculture to cause attendance to be low. In 1903, it is noted, "the Gower Company of the Glamorgan Imperial Yeomanry starting this afternoon for their annual drill in

Troop camp of the Gower Yeomanry.
Ivor Parry, Llanrhidian, is standing, 8th from left.

Margam, a few children of this school went over to Reynoldston to see them off."

Local fairs also proved an attraction to the children, for example, Reynoldston Christmas Fat Stock Fair on the 11th December 1905, the 1st Annual Agricultural Show at Penrice Park on the 20th September 1906, and Gowerton Flannel and Pleasure Fair on the 6th September 1915, were all responsible for continuing absenteeism. Several scholars were again absent in 1915, when a circus came to Reynoldston.

In the 1920s, these distractions continued – 23rd September 1920, "blackberrying accounts for the absence of several children lately," and "sheep washing and shearing caused the absence of some scholars." Even Sunday school excursions were responsible for low attendance, for although there was a holiday on the 26th July 1921 so that the Sunday school could go to Porthcawl in charabancs, the log book reproachfully notes on the 27th July: "the excursionists were very late arriving home yesterday evening. As a result the attendance, especially in the forenoon was poor."

The lack of attendance was obviously a concern to Miss Dodds when she was headmistress in the 1890s. She notes on the 20th January 1893 that a Committee was called this week to consider the matter of "Attendance at School" but "only one member put in an appearance, so of course, nothing was done!"

Even the teachers themselves found regular attendance difficult. A disapproving entry on the 1st February 1903 notes: "Miss Williams absented herself from school this afternoon. It seems that she went down to Llanmadoc to see a stranded steamer." Nothing, however, compares with the tribulations of Miss Ann and Miss Dorothy Trounsell in attempting to carry out their duties.

23rd Sept. 1907: "Miss Trounsell absent. She generally returns to her home in Loughor for the weekend, and the high tide which covered the road between Loughor and Gowerton prevented her from returning."

13th January 1908: "Miss Trounsell absent. She missed her train."

31st Aug./1st Sept. 1908: "Miss Trounsell absent – detained at her home by the great storm."

12th October 1908: "Miss Trounsell absent. The high tide prevented her from returning from her home in Loughor."

10th March 1913: "Miss Trounsell absent. She generally cycles home to Llanelly for the weekend. In returning to duty this Monday a.m. the high tide covered portions of the road between Loughor and Gowerton and in trying to ride through the water she fell into it and was completely soaked and returned to Llanelly."

Occasionally the school was closed through illness, as on the 16th January 1896: "school closed for a fortnight today, owing to measles," and from Jan. 18th-5th Feb. 1906: "the school closed – whooping cough."

On the 3rd Feb. it is noted with disapproval: "poor attendance through a scare caused by a false rumour that a family was suffering from the 'Itch'. The parents took their children to the Doctor to be examined. He certified that they were not suffering from anything of the kind."

Punishments included, for a falsehood, writing on a slate: "Dare to be true, nothing can need a lie" and a stroke of the rod for quarrelling on the way to school. Two boys were sent home on the 26th Feb. 1887 because their father had not paid their school fees, and many lost their attendance mark through late arrival. On the 29th May 1907, Richard Kenneth Williams, an infant, was sent home because he had swallowed a marble – and his attendance mark was cancelled.

School Memories

Wilma Collins remembers . . .
My mother, Mary Austin and her sister Annie were in school on the 27th June 1906, when an earth tremor shook Swansea, and was felt in Llanrhidian. The children were in the classroom when the partition that

Llanrhidian School 1907.
Back row: Miss Evans, Tom Rees (Cillibion), Ambrose Austin (Newton Farm), Trevor Austin (The Hollies), Arthur Dunn (Cillibion), Miss Trounsell, Harry Beynon (Llethrid Farm), Mr. James.
Middle row: Lewis Eaton, Maud Eaton, Emeline Lewis, Evelyn Harry and Gladys Harry (Leason), Daisy Williams, ?, Arthur Lewis.
Front Row: Mansfred Grove (Leason), Tom Eaton, Edgar Williams, Gordon Harry (Lane House), Kenny Williams, Harry Davies, Tom Tucker (The Common), Doris Harry, ?.

Kenny Williams, "an infant, who was sent home on the 29th May 1907 because he had swallowed a marble", is in the front row, 5th from right.

divided the infants from the main school, shook violently. The children were punished for causing the disturbance.

On Dick Beynon's first day at school, he listened while his friends told their teacher their names. They all had a middle name! "And what's your name?" he was asked. Not wanting to be left out, he replied confidently, "Richard Dick Beynon!" "Don't be silly!" said his teacher crossly.

Whilst playing paper chase with his cousin John Williams, Dick was struck on the head by a stone that was loosened by John as he climbed over a wall. Staggering home slightly concussed, Dick's mother made him lie down, and pulled the curtains to keep out the sunshine. Not long afterwards the Headmaster arrived. The children, passing Dick's house, had seen the drawn curtains, and told him that Dick was dead!

SCHOOLDAYS IN LLANRHIDIAN

Llanrhidian School, 1932.
From the rear, left to right: Glyn Clement, Frank Jones.
Pearl Williams, Averil Austin, Audrey Williams, Ismay Williams, Glenis Grove, Hilda Thomas, Meg Morgan, Peggy Morgan, Wilma Grove, Iris Pearce, Doris Clement.
Ronald Morgan (Common), Ronald Morgan, William Grove, Reggie Pearce, Freddie Williams, Olive Clement, Brenda Jones.
Terry Williams, Selwyn Beynon, Ronald Jones.

Audrey Williams remembers . . .
We always took sandwiches and a can of tea for lunch – no school dinners in those days! There was a large black range in the headmaster's room, and it was on this range that we placed our cans of tea to keep them warm.

Janie Hutin remembers . . .
My uncle, Brynley Dunn and his friends wouldn't go to school on Fridays as the boys had to do knitting then. His mother went to see the headmaster, who couldn't understand why the boys had to learn to knit either, and he stopped the classes. The boys returned!

Nancy Payne remembers . . .
We lived in Pengwern Farm, and when I was five years old I would walk three miles every day to Llanrhidian School. My mother would take me as far as the stile, as I was too small to climb over it, and then off I would go with my can of tea and sandwiches.

Ivy Griffiths remembers . . .
I remember my first day at school. The teacher, Miss M. Lewis, wrote a note to my mother asking if she minded if the teacher called me by my second name, Doreen, because she preferred that name. So I was known as Doreen throughout my school days in Llanrhidian, and some of those pupils who knew me then call me Doreen to this very day.

Eric Morgan remembers . . .
To start and finish every day we had "Hands together, eyes closed . . ." When I had a little peep once, I saw Miss Davies putting LIPSTICK on – which was very daring of her!

In the boys' yard, we played cars with old tyres, which we whipped with our hands or a stick. We hated what I suppose was called "physical training". We were marched around the yard performing right wheels, about turns, etc. – a relic of the 19th century which had mostly died out by the 1920s.

WELL-REMEMBERED VOICES

In May 1986, Eric Morgan tape-recorded conversations with some of Llanrhidian's older residents, including his mother, Violet Morgan. Here are some of their memories of their schooldays.

Mrs. Violet Morgan . . .
When I started school, I was in the old school at first. It was just one long room, but then a partition was added, which divided the infants from the other classes. The infants would sit around the "babies' table" – a long oblong table with small chairs around it.

We sat at long desks, with the Master's chair facing us. There was a modulator (tonic sol-fa chart) on the board behind him, and maps on the walls. He wrote the attendance each day on the board in chalk. The "Whipper In" would come occasionally to check on us. The Master was very strict, and often used the cane. I remember Jim Brockie put a small fish he had caught into the Master's pocket. He had a hammering for that! We used to go down to Uncle Jack's (Hill House) to eat our dinner. There were so many of us there, they wouldn't have enough chairs for us all, and we had to stand up around the table. We would buy a 3d loaf, and take butter and eggs that they would boil for us. The children who stayed in school for dinner had to sit at their desks to eat their food. The older boys were often up to mischief. I remember that they put a goose down the chimney of the school, and one day they used George Thomas's ropes to tie up the school door, and we couldn't get out!

We would walk to school from Leason, but on wet days when Leason Pool was up, my father would take us in the horse and trap. At playtime, we would go out onto the hill, until Mr. James blew his whistle. "Whistle's gone," we would say.

Mary and Margaret Harry would clean the school and light the fires.

Miss Mary O'Keefe . . .
I went to the new school. Mr. James, the Master, was very strict. He kept a cane by his desk, and would hit it against the wood. He lived in the village, and if a boy passed him and didn't doff his cap, he would be punished the next day.

The infants would sit at the big table playing with clay and paints. There was a large counting frame with coloured beads on an easel in front of the class, and on the walls were portraits of Owain Glyndŵr and Edith Cavell. In the lower classes, we wrote with slates and slate pencils. I felt very posh when we left them behind. The powdered ink was mixed with water, and then the Master would come around with a brown bottle to fill up our inkwells. They had brass tops, and we would take in a rag to polish the brass. It was a matter of pride to have the brightest one! Paraffin lamps lighted the school – you would have to pull a chain down to light them, and in the roof was a ventilator.

I would wear thick black stockings and boots, and of course, a pinafore.

They were made of calico or linen, with a square yoke. I would have to change into my play pinafore when I went home. My coat hanger number in the cloakroom was number 54. We weren't allowed to stay in the cloakrooms at playtime. Whatever the weather we would have to go to the play shed. It was as cold as charity there! We played hopscotch and ring games. In class, we did a lot of mental arithmetic and silent reading.

Kenny Williams . . .
I passed the scholarship for Gowerton School, and would leave home on a Monday about seven o'clock, and would walk to Llanmorlais station to catch the train there. Then I was in lodgings all week until Friday evening when I would catch the train home again.

2

World War I

Arthur Lewis, Llanrhidian.

*Gower Church Magazine, December 1914, Parish of Llanrhidian . . .
Gifts. We thank Mrs. Dix, of Stavel Hagar for the gift of a well-made shirt of Welsh flannel, which will no doubt be appreciated by the soldier who receives it. All the shirts, ten in number, made through the kindness of Llanrhidian ladies, are now complete. There is a strong feeling in favour of sending the shirts to the Gower Convalescent Home, if they are required.*

The hospital at Horton.

Eric Morgan writes . . .

Violet Davies (later Morgan) and Annie Austin (later Williams) both volunteered as part-time nurses in World War I, joining the Voluntary Aid Detachment (VAD) of the Red Cross. They did spells of duty at the hospital at Horton – a very large house, converted for the purpose. The wounded soldiers there had already received treatment and were placed at Horton for care and recuperation.

In a recorded conversation with her son Eric, Violet recalled going in to Ben Evans in Swansea (a very posh shop, she remembers, which had the contract to supply uniforms), to buy her long navy nurse's coat, and being greeted by a 'shopwalker' who was wearing a dress with a yard-long train! Annie Phillips, a seamstress who lived in Millbrook Cottage, Llanrhidian, made her three uniforms and a dozen aprons with red crosses sewed on them.

Soldiers and nurses at Horton. Violet Morgan is standing on the left.

Authorisation to wear a Red Cross uniform.

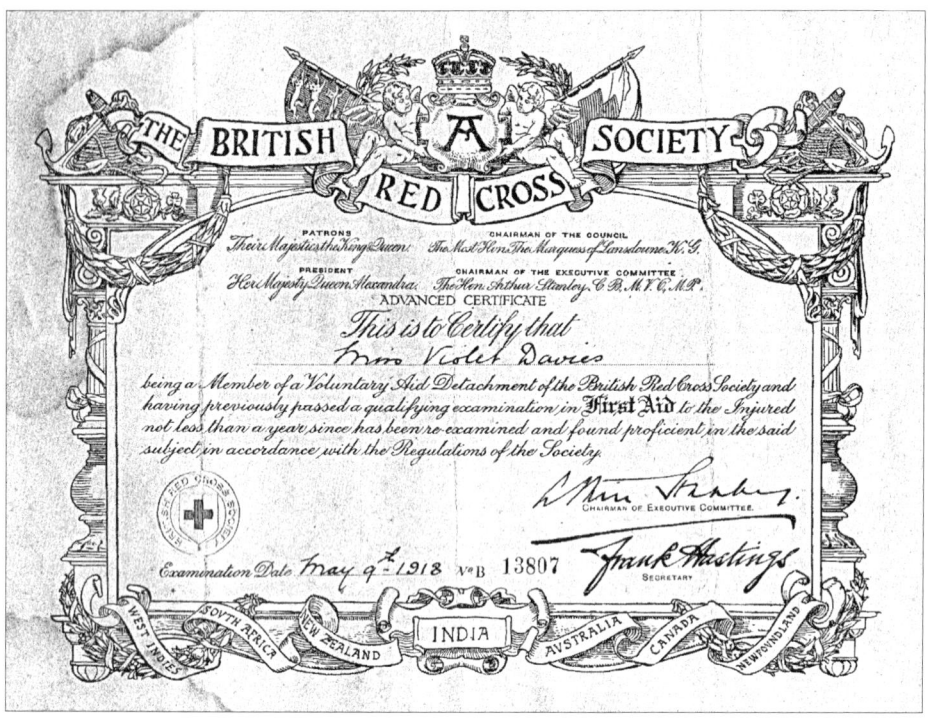

Violet Morgan's VAD certificate.

Right: Violet Morgan.

Bottom: Nurses at Horton.
Annie Austin is in the row on the right,
with her head slightly bowed.

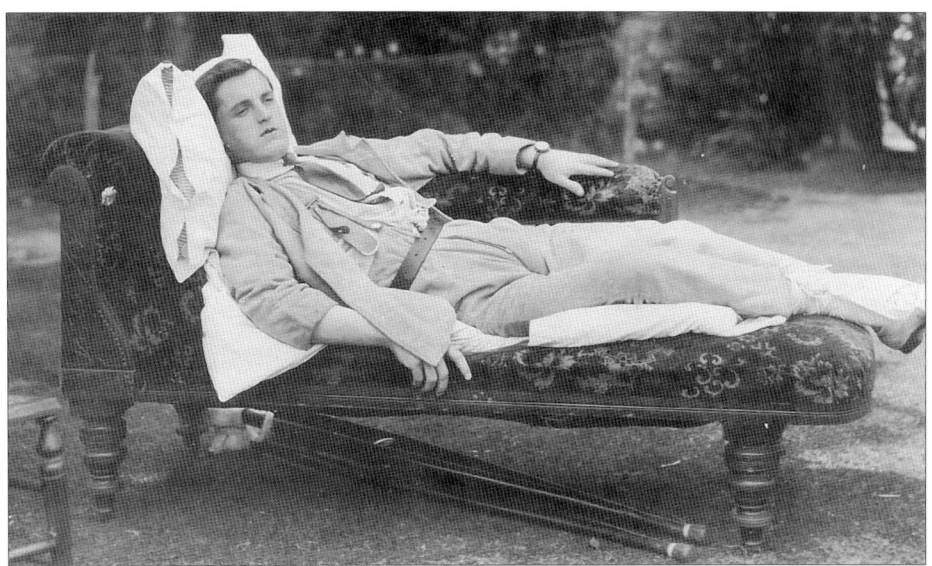

A wounded soldier, Horton.

```
TELEGRAMS: ESTATE, REYNOLDSTON.
TELEPHONE: 7, REYNOLDSTON.
                                        ESTATE OFFICE.
                                        PENRICE CASTLE.
                                        REYNOLDSTON, R.S.O.
                                                  GLAMORGANSHIRE.

                                        20th January, 1919.

Miss Violet Davies,
    Leaston,
        REYNOLDSTON.

Dear Miss Davies,
            At the last Meeting of the Hospital House Committee
it was unanimously decided to ask you to accept the enclosed
cheque for £1. 1. 0. as an honorarium for the assistance which
you so ably rendered to the Committee during the last week of
demobilisation of the Hospital.  The Committee fully recognise
that the work on which you were engaged could not strictly be
asked of you as a member of the V.A.D., and they therefore
appreciate all the more the assistance you were good enough to
give them.
                    Yours faithfully,

                    Hopkin Pritchard

                                Hon. Sec. & Commandant.
```

Demobilisation of the hospital.
Hopkin Pritchard was the estate manager of the Penrice Estate until the 1930s.
He was famed for riding a white horse – and for being greatly feared –
in days when a tenant could be turned out for poaching!

WILL MORGAN
HMS *DUKE OF EDINBURGH*, BATTLE OF JUTLAND
Written by Eric Morgan

Will Morgan's whole period of service was spent on the heavy armoured cruiser, *Duke of Edinburgh*, that was normally based at Scapa Flow, but also used Rosyth and Devonport. It sailed from Liverpool on transatlantic voyages to New York and Novia Scotia and on at least one occasion had a cargo of gold bullion.

The *Duke* was one of a squadron of four, along with *Defence* the flagship, *Warrior* and *Black Prince*. In the battle of Jutland – the biggest ever sea battle – the squadron was ordered to steam up the North Sea between the British and German battle fleets, though the High Command, under Beatty, complained that they impaired visibility with their smoke – the ships were coal fired.

The Germans found their range, and first sank the *Defence* with the squadron's admiral, Arbuthnot. *Warrior* and *Black Prince* suffered the same fate. The *Duke of Edinburgh*'s captain turned through 90 degrees, and steamed west at full speed – just 9 knots, disobeying the orders of the dead admiral. Will thought that the captain was court-martialled for that action.

However, a ship and its eight hundred men lived to see 1st June 1916 – and the rest of their lives.

WORLD WAR I

HMS Duke of Edinburgh.

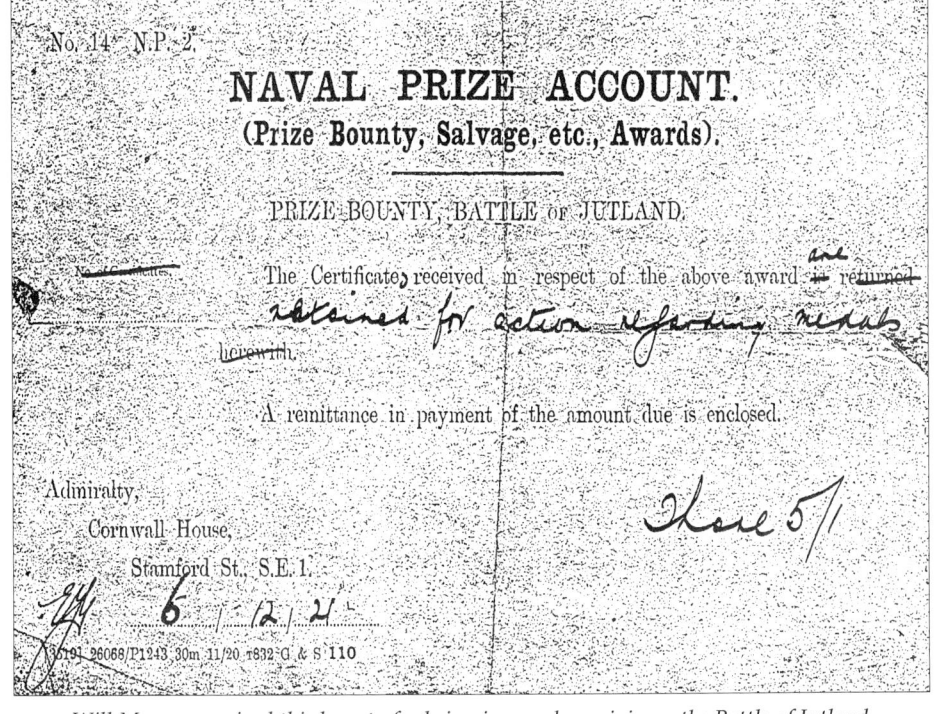

Will Morgan received this bounty for being in – and surviving – the Battle of Jutland. Pay at the time was about 9 old pence a day.

George Tucker, Able Seaman, Wales/Z/3713
s.s. *Inniscarra*, Royal Naval Volunteer Reserve

Remembered by Eric Tucker

In the First World War, villages whose men all returned home safely were called 'Thankful Villages'. There were only forty-three 'Thankful Villages' in Great Britain.

George Tucker was the only member of Llanrhidian parish to lose his life in the First World War. He was killed when his ship the S.S. *Inniscarra* was sunk without warning by a German submarine off the south coast of Ireland on the 12th May 1918. He was twenty years old, and a total of 28 crew were killed following the sinking of the *Inniscarra*, but the captain, H. Hore, survived.

George was the son of Charles and Martha Tucker, Rock House, Llanrhidian, and his name is on the Plymouth Naval Memorial overlooking the Hoe in Plymouth, and on a plaque over the vestry door at Ebenezer Chapel, Oldwalls, where he is described as dying "a hero's death, standing by his gun until the last."

Marjorie Williams recalls . . .
My father, Parry Williams of Baytree House, served with the Gower Yeomanry in France during World War I. He sent many cards from the trenches to his family in Llanrhidian (*see colour pages*).

Parry Williams.

Sidney Williams (standing, 2nd from right) was in the Welsh Pioneers, and served in Salonika.

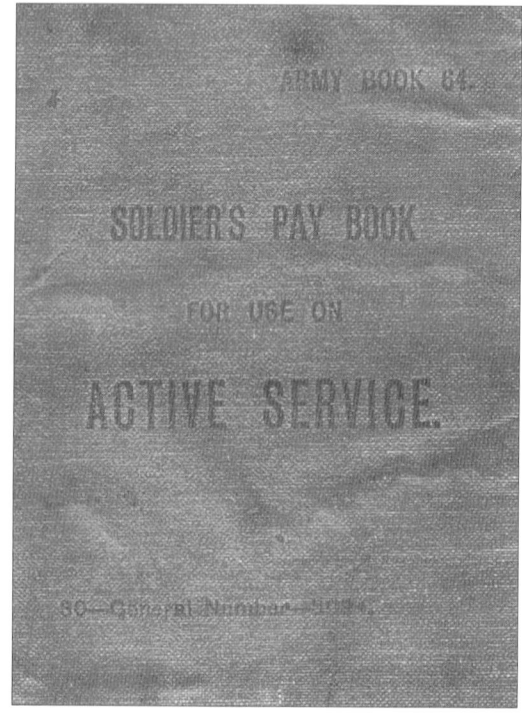

Sidney Williams's pay book.

WORLD WAR I

Soldiers' Will Form, 1914.

Olwen Williams, Sidney's sister (back row, 3rd from right), worked in an ammunition factory in Burry Port during World War I.

*Frank Jones was in the Royal Artillery,
and served in the trenches in France.*

*On the back of this photograph of the 'Grantully Castle', Frank Jones had written:
"This is the ship I sailed home in."*

WORLD WAR I

Dick Dunn, Hill House, joined the Royal Engineers, and served in East Africa.

Arthur Dunn, Cillibion.

ALBERT WILLIAMS, PANT GLAS
Remembered by Audrey Williams

My father served in the Royal Engineers during the First World War, and was in the midst of some terrible battles. I remember my mother telling me how he described to her his experiences and what he witnessed at Ypres.

Being a country boy, he used a country analogy. "It was like watching a reaper and binder in a cornfield, cutting down great swathes of corn, in the same way our soldiers fell like the corn."

However, he came home at the end of the war after serving four years in the army.

3

World War II

Sergeant Ivor Llewellyn Thomas, alongside his aircraft.

The Thomas Family, Mount Pleasant Farm

Sergeant Ivor Llewellyn Thomas.

The Thomas family, Mount Pleasant Farm (George Ivor and his wife Annie Maria Thomas), lost their two sons in the Second World War. Albert was in the army, and Ivor an RAF pilot.

Sergeant Ivor Llewellyn Thomas, 580177, 40SQD Royal Air Force, died on Friday, 10th May 1940, aged 24, in Holland. Three planes, including Ivor's, were sent over the Maginot Line as a gesture to the advancing Germans, and Ivor's plane was shot down.

Ivor was married to Joyce Thomas of Peterborough. During his time in the RAF (which Ivor joined as a career airman before the war), Ivor would sweep low over Llanrhidian Marsh in his Blenheim bomber, and then would just crest the top of the hill. Marjorie Williams remembers being terrified when he did this one morning when she was on her way to school. Ivor's grave is in The Hague (Westduin), Holland, cared for by a Dutch family who have stayed in touch with his sister Ivy Griffiths, and the families have exchanged visits. Ivor's grave reference is Allied Plot Row 1, grave 7.

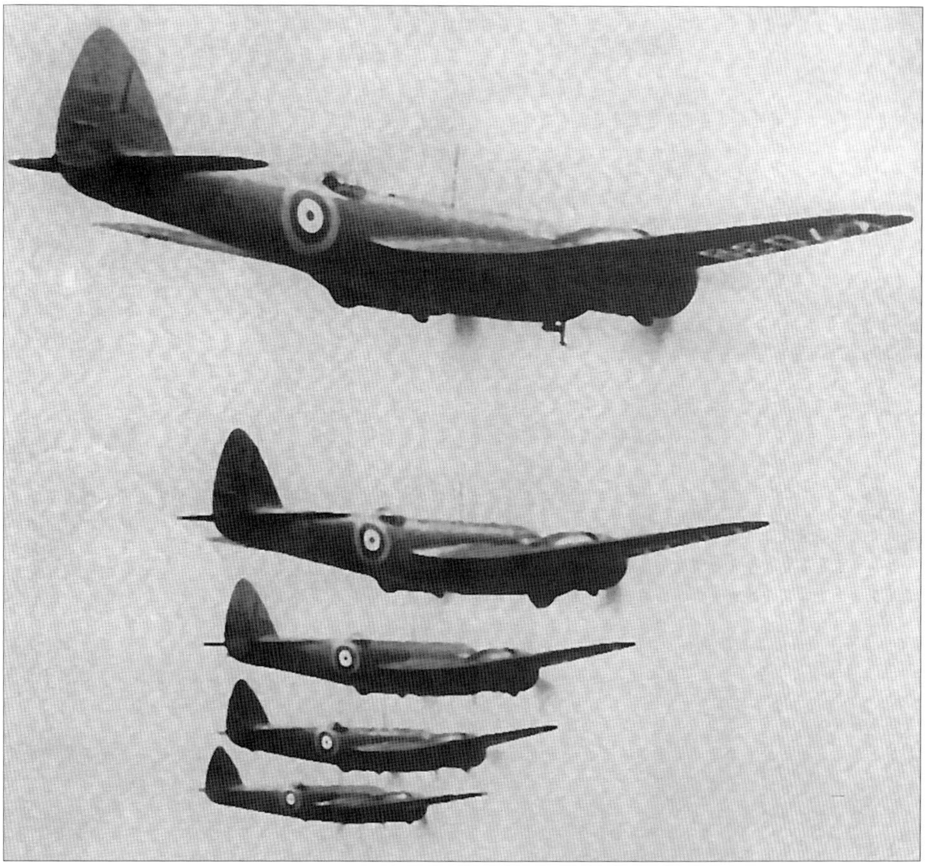

WORLD WAR II

A Christmas card sent by Ivor to his parents from RAF Wyton.

Ivor, front row, 4th from left, with his squadron.

Gunner Albert George Thomas, 1609017, 79 (The Hertfordshire Yeomanry), HAA Regiment, Royal Artillery, died on Thursday, 21st September 1944, aged 27. Albert, who was his colonel's driver, died from shock when a shrapnel bomb exploded alongside his car in Italy – there was not a mark on his body when he was found. Albert is buried in Florence War Cemetery. His grave reference is 1. H. 3.

Gunner Albert George Thomas.

Florence War Cemetery.

Gower Church Magazine, Parish of Llanrhidian. Sept. 1941 . . .
Mr. and Mrs. Oliver Grove have received news that their son Ernie is reported "Missing." We hope that good news will reach them soon.

Gower Church Magazine, Parish of Llanrhidian. Dec. 1941 . . .
Congratulations to Mr. and Mrs. O. Grove, that their son Ernie is safe and well. He is a prisoner-of-war.

Ernie's Story

In the 1930s, Ernie Grove's father said to him, "There's a little man in Europe called Hitler, and he's causing a bit of trouble. I think it would be a good idea to get a job on the land." He was hoping that this meant that Ernie would not be called up to join the army. So Ernie began working for a farmer in Tycoch. One day, the farmer said to him, "ERRRNIE! I've had a letter about you!" "About me?" said Ernie, "I've never had a letter in my life!" The farmer had had a letter from the War Office informing him that he had one too many workers for the acreage of the farm, so Ernie had to go to war.

He joined an artillery regiment, and was posted to Rhyl, where there was a large artillery camp. Later he was posted to Woolwich, London where one of his duties was to act as guard in a hospital for wounded Luftwaffe prisoners. Eventually he was sent to North Africa, where he saw enemy action, including being strafed by German fighter planes. Soon after being posted to Crete, the Germans invaded the island, and many military personnel were captured, Ernie included.

Then began a journey through Greece and the Balkans, arriving eventually at his first prisoner-of-war camp, Genshagen.

The uniforms with which the soldiers had been issued in North Africa were unsuitable for the cold German climate, so the men were given French uniforms, and Ernie, because he had a foot injury, was given Dutch clogs to wear. The soldiers were moved to various camps; one was an ex-railway station, where they worked clearing the tracks of snow, but one of the squaddies defaced a picture of Hitler, and they were again moved on. At last, he arrived at Zittau, where he worked in an opencast mine.

Genshagen. Ernie Grove is kneeling in the front row, 3rd from left.

Zittau. Ernie is sixth from left.

When returning from work, the men crossed tracks with Ukrainian women prisoners returning from their work in the fields. One man drew an onion, and a picture of a railway track, and pushed it through the wire fence around the women's camp with some Red Cross chocolate. The women would then drop an occasional onion on the tracks in return for chocolate, and the men would enjoy onion soup.

During the latter stages of the war, American bombers could be regularly seen with their fighter escorts, and they bombed the area where Ernie worked. Mainly civilians now supervised the prisoners, with just a few soldiers. One civilian, an old man, said: "Listen!" They could hear the distant sound of artillery. "Americans!" he whispered. The prisoners were then moved east, away from the Americans, sleeping rough by the roadside. Ernie and some of his colleagues decided to escape, confident that the German guards, knowing the end of the war was in sight, would not look for them. His friend there, who came from St. Thomas, Swansea, decided not to take the risk, but asked Ernie, in the event of his getting back home safely, to let his family know that he was well. The men hid in a copse for a while, and then decided to head back to the camp. They discovered a mineshaft, with a ladder leading down. Inside they found a German, whose job it was to man the pumps. This man returned home that night, but assured them that he would not divulge to anyone that they were there, saying, "Don't worry, it's over!"

Arriving back in camp, it was an emotional moment for Ernie to see a tank with the Stars and Stripes flying from its turret. Ernie was eventually repatriated, and, as promised, contacted his friend's family. His friend arrived home six weeks later, and still visits Ernie occasionally to reminisce.

Ernie returned to work on the farm. The farmer greeted him one day with, "ERRRNIE! I've had another letter for you!" "What colour is it?" asked Ernie. "Brown." he replied. "That's it!" said Ernie, "They want me back!" And they did! Ernie had to report for training before being sent to the Far East. During his training, the men (all ex-POWs) were lined up, and an officer went down the line tapping a few men on their shoulders. Ernie's shoulder was tapped. The officer told the men that instead of going to the Far East, they were off to Buckingham Palace! During the weeks of training, Hiroshima and Nagasaki had been bombed, and the war was almost over, so Ernie, instead of going out east, was off to a garden party.

When talking to Ernie, he always emphasises how lucky he was, in spite of a few shrapnel wounds, to be able to return home fit and well, unlike some of his closest village friends.

Fritz's Story

Fritz Olstersdorf was born in Heiligenbeil, East Prussia, and was one of twelve children, ten girls and two boys. He was twelve when World War II started. His hometown became a garrison, and Fritz remembers lying on his back in the local sports ground, watching planes flying back and forth to Poland.

As the war progressed, the Russians were approaching from the east, but the Nazis had forbidden anyone to leave East Prussia. At the last moment they allowed civilians to leave, and in their millions they did.

Everyone had to pack up what they could carry, and head towards Germany, the more fortunate on horses and carts, the rest walking. Fritz left before his mother and sisters, as the young men had to help the refugees cross a narrow strip of land called the Frisches Haff, which was only 8 to 10 kms wide, and surrounded by the Baltic. The weather was bitterly cold, and many people and horses drowned as they slipped into the frozen water. Fritz's mother and sisters were put aboard a boat and taken across the Baltic to Germany.

Fritz eventually reached Germany where, as the situation in Berlin became more desperate, young and old were enlisted into the army to defend Berlin to the last man. At 17 years of age, Fritz was enlisted. He spent three weeks in the trenches, where he caught a severe chest infection, and was taken to hospital. Whilst there, with the approach of the Allies, the hospital was evacuated. Soon, the Russians arrived in Berlin and the war was over.

Fritz was now a prisoner-of-war, and taken with the other prisoners by transport trucks to Belgium. There he was put in a camp of a few thousand prisoners, where they were used as unpaid labour. He stayed there until 1st March 1946, when he was transferred with approximately sixty other prisoners to Chepstow, and then on to a camp in Scurlage. Fritz remembers how, after being so hungry in Belgium, he couldn't get enough of the food there – managing to consume six bowls of pea soup in one sitting!

In 1947, Fritz went to work at Stembridge Farm with Mr. and Mrs. Tanner, recalling that it was a hot and beautiful summer as he cut corn in the fields, but the winter was severe, and he helped clear the snow off the roads from Scurlage to Porteynon.

At Christmas time, in 1948, the prisoners were allowed to return to Germany for a holiday. They could then choose if they wanted to stay in Germany or return to Wales. Fritz had met Dulcie Lewis, Llanrhidian, in a dance in the village hall, and chose to return to Gower. When Dulcie asked him why he had returned, he replied romantically, "To fetch my accordion!"

In the meantime, Fritz's family had been searching for him, and he received a letter from them. In 1948, when he returned to Germany he was able to see them again, although one of his sisters was missing and not heard of again.

On the 24th December 1948, Fritz received his official release papers, and his naturalization papers in 1953.

Emrys's Story

In 1940, Emrys Dunn was called to the YMCA in Swansea for a medical examination and then was enlisted in the South Wales Borderers. He was sent to Brecon for basic training. The soldiers were tested on their ability to fire a rifle. As Emrys was going up to take his turn, one soldier said to him, "Don't hit the target too often, or they'll make you a sniper." So Emrys missed a few. He attended two courses at the end of the training course, one in mine laying, and the other in laying booby traps. Emrys scored 97% for booby trap laying and was promoted to Lance Corporal of Platoon B, and stayed on to help train the next batch of soldiers.

Emrys Dunn.   *Emrys in Abyssinia.*

One day, Emrys and some friends read in Platoon Orders that the RASC wanted truck drivers, so they, deciding that they would prefer driving to walking, applied. Emrys, whose experience of driving was restricted to a baby Austin, found himself behind the wheel of a 10-ton lorry. He was then posted to Lydden near Dover, a command depot with an enormous stock of all types of lorries, where he was employed driving shells to the gun emplacements in Dover. He was later transferred to Arsenal in London, prior to being sent to Norway. However, he contracted laryngitis and spent some time in the military hospital, and when he had recovered, his unit had already left. He was sent to Chelmsford and then on to Liverpool, eventually boarding the s.s. *Mauritania* with 7,000 others, en route for Egypt.

They sailed in a convoy of 22 ships, sleeping in hammocks slung in the hold. They occasionally had lifeboat drills, which became somewhat chaotic as all the men tried to get on deck at the same time. On arriving in Durban, South Africa, the men stayed in a holding camp for two weeks. Emrys enjoyed his time there, the camp was near a beach, the South Africans were generous, and welcoming – the soldiers never had to pay for their drinks there. They then boarded another ship and arrived at a holding camp in Cairo.

The men were now dressed in desert uniform. Here Emrys was assigned to 233 Company RASC, supplying the troops at El Alamein with food, petrol and guns, feeding the dumps of stores behind the lines there. The noise was incredible, as Montgomery had ordered continual bombardment of the enemy. The men were pulled out of the line occasionally for a two-week break, and Emrys was able to visit the Pyramids. Emrys contracted amoebic dysentery and was sent to the 6th Australian General Hospital, which he remembers as a marvellous place with good food, chocolates, and nurses from Melbourne. He stayed there for six weeks, his weight dropping from 10s 7lbs, to 6 stone. He then went to Nathania in Palestine to recuperate. He was there for six months, and was able to visit Nazareth, Jerusalem and the Garden of Gethsemane. In Palestine, he stayed at Toc H.

Fit once more, Emrys had a stroke of luck. He was posted to a civilian company in Abyssinia, where twenty or so soldiers were in charge of the Arab drivers, as some of the personnel had been called back to France. Here, Emrys would carry messages by motorbike. He was then promoted to QMS and was in charge of supplies.

The day that they heard that the War had ended was a wonderful day, and the men went 'a bit daft', and as there was little discipline, the colonel decided to have a polo match between officers and NCOs – on donkeys! The colonel sat on his motionless donkey in the goal, whilst everyone else tried, without much success, to get his donkey to move.

Emrys was demobbed in 1946, sailing home on the s.s. *Awati*, calling in Greece to pick up some war brides. Special facilities had to be provided for them on board – including a round-the-clock guard.

Dick's Story

After an interview and medical in Penarth, Dick Beynon joined the RAF. He attended training in Bournemouth, Skegness and Gloucester and was then sent to Cardington where the R101 was built. He went to a maintenance unit, where he delivered vehicles and parts, and collected vehicles from factories. One course he attended taught how to waterproof vehicles. After waterproofing a four-ton truck, Dick had to drive it underwater – so he made sure that he had done a good job first!

Dick Beynon.

When "lease and lend" came in to operation, Dick worked in Cardiff, helping to put together vehicles that had been crated over from America; he then distributed them to airfields around the UK. He became a driver for his CO, Wing Commander West, who always referred to him as 'Laddie', but he was unable to stay as his driver for long as his possession of an HGV licence meant he was needed to drive heavy equipment.

In Gloucester, one of Dick's room-mates was a Brummie called 'Toothless' who was always miserable. When he was out one day, Dick had his bed hoisted up on a crane outside the hut, and on returning, 'Toothless' reported his missing bed to the RAF police. Luckily, it was their own duty officer who came to deal with the problem, and went straight up to Dick and said, "Come on, Ianto, where's his bed?" Dick indicated that it was outside, and the officer turned to see it swinging in the wind from a crane.

Another of Dick's colleagues was Dai Jenkins from Ewenny Potteries, who claimed that he could tap dance, so he was encouraged to climb on the table to give an exhibition. He did so, and put on quite a show, but spoiled it by falling off the table and breaking his ankle. He was always known afterwards as 'The Welsh Tap Dancer'.

Dick carried one photograph with him throughout the war – it was a photo of Dick himself with his uncle in the Gower Show with three winning horses, but the word 'Gower' had to be cut out, as he was not allowed to carry anything that would show where he lived.

For twelve months before D Day, the service men realised that 'something big' was coming up, and deduced from the amount of waterproofing that they had to do, that it would be at sea. Before D Day, all service men involved in the Expeditionary Force were given a letter from Eisenhower.

For four days, thousands of landing craft were off the Isle of Wight, waiting for the weather to improve. Dick's landing craft with two lorries and a crane on board was amongst them. The men were on 'iron rations' – dog biscuits Dick called them, with a bar of chocolate, but the sailors shared their rations with them. The day before D Day, wearing their Mae Wests, the craft and crew set off. Surrounded by destroyers and minesweepers, the six men on Dick's boat tried to sleep. The craft hit a buoy, and instantly, in an act of self-preservation, the six sleeping men were up and charging through the door!

The craft arrived at Arromanches, Normandy, and Dick's job in 551 Forward Repair Unit was to recover crashed aircraft. Spitfires and Hurricanes would often land with little damage done to them, and they would be sent back to Britain for repair. Dick saw the 1,000-bomber raid

Dick at the Gower Show.

on Caen, which was still in the possession of the Germans. The raid took place in daylight, and the men were able to see the bombs dropping. Later, seeing one plane land, Dick went towards it and the pilot climbed out – he was a German, but fortunately surrendered immediately.

After advancing into Germany, Dick was sent to the Far East. He was kitted out in England to go to Burma, but was instead sent by boat to Bombay, and then drafted to central India, where many anti-British riots were taking place. Dick and his colleagues were travelling down one road, and met a riot. An American had driven through the crowd earlier, and had been burnt to death. Dick realised what was happening and executed what came to be described as "the fastest three point turn in the east!" Dick does not have good memories of his time in India, and was glad to leave; describing the finest sight that he saw as "Bombay from the blunt end of a ship!" On leaving India, the men had a choice of flying home or travelling by boat. He chose a boat – as did most of the air force personnel!

Dick was demobbed at Preston – and took a week to reach home, after a variety of celebrations.

Leonard P. Collins. R.A.F.
H.M.S. *Courageous*

This is Leonard's own account of the sinking of HMS *Courageous*.

When in September 1939, I was posted to the aircraft carrier *Courageous* as a flight mechanic, I felt some concern about my inadequacy as a swimmer. The sight of *Courageous* restored my confidence – what could possibly happen to a ship of that size? On September 17th, the *Courageous* was guarding the trade routes in the Atlantic, travelling a zigzag course to cheat any lurking submarines of their prey. The carrier however had to maintain a straight course when planes were landing on the flight deck. It was a fine evening, and the last aircraft, a Swordfish, No. k8346, had landed and was taken down by lift to the hangar on sea level. It was in position ready for the rigger to lash her securely. Word came that the carrier's escorting destroyers had gone to help against an attack on a distant merchant ship. My immediate job was to drain the oil from the Swordfish's engine, and as I went to the rear of the hangar to find some empty cans, I noticed that the steel doors had dropped to darken the ship. I carried on with my work . . . and then it came! The deafening explosion! The sheet of flame from the vicinity of the steel door! The shuddering of the mighty vessel as she keeled over!

Leonard P. Collins.

Striving to keep on my feet I gasped to a fellow worker, "What was that?"

"Seems like a torpedo, mate."

We stumbled to the steel doors to find they had split from top to bottom. I caught hold of one side of the split and forced the other side with my foot. One by one the men could squeeze through until I was left trying to hold the split apart to get through myself. Panting with exertion, I wondered, "What now?"

It was then I became aware of my hands, ripped and bleeding from tearing at the steel doors. The sound of toolboxes, empty cans and loose parts being hurled violently added to the crashes of the planes breaking their lashings inside the hangar.

I found that I was on the officers' deck, where men were trying to bring guns to bear on the sub. An officer, with his fingers in his ears, kept shouting, "Man overboard!" and it occurred to me that with the ship keeling over at a crazy angle, it was only a matter of time before we would all be in the water, struggling for our lives. Instinctively, my one thought was to get to the lower deck as quickly as possible. Others had the same idea, although it seemed almost impossible. It was like climbing a ladder, the going was hard, and the man above me shouted "I'm going to jump from here!" I was unable to turn to see how he fared, but I never saw him again. Some men had been jumping into the sea only to hit the side of the ship, whilst others lay spread-eagled across the guns having been killed immediately. When I reached the flight deck, a young man came stumbling towards me saying, "What are you going to do?" "Well, I can't swim – there's not much point in jumping in." I was hoping that somewhere there would be a functional lifeboat or float, but much of the emergency equipment had failed us, and the life rafts were stuck to the side of the ship with paint. This was the last time that life rafts were painted with the ship.

"Come on, Ginge," he replied, "I'll look after you!" With that the ship gave a sickening lurch and my companion was in the water yelling, "Come on, man, jump!" The urgency in his voice increased as I stripped off most of my clothes. There was a packet of Woodbine in my overall pocket, which I carefully removed to my side pocket. Then I rolled up my shoes in my overall and laid them neatly on the deck. Now the choice was for me to jump or stay on board until the ship went down. I jumped! The sea was choppy, full of men and loose timber, and from the many faces around me I recognised the man who had undertaken to look after me. I immediately grabbed hold of him, but it was clear that his chance of survival would be slim with my clawing, clutching weight, so I stayed away from him and lost him in the confusion. My attempt at swimming was to try to elbow myself out of the water, whilst striving to reach one of the logs. It seemed futile, but struggling desperately I finally reached one. The log was spinning rapidly in the water, so that each time I took hold of it, the spin would force me back into the water, causing me agonising stomach pains as I swallowed more water. Eventually I was able to steady the log and get a respite. Exhausted, I lifted my head wearily to look around. Then I saw the *Courageous* silhouetted against the evening sky, a mighty ship slowly sinking, her 'Red Duster' still flying defiantly. It was then that I picked out a lonely figure, saw him stiffen into a semblance of standing to attention. I saw him salute the flag, and then throw his peaked cap on the waves. It was a sight that produced a strange mixture of emotions, where awe, fear, pity and sadness mingled confusingly.

My thoughts were suddenly jerked back to the problem of survival, for I was near enough to be caught in the suction. I was dragged struggling down through the water, until I thought that my lungs would burst. It was then that I thought that the end was near. I stopped struggling. A sense of peace came over me, a freedom from pain, and calmly I wondered what my folks would think. It would be in the local paper. What would the heading be? Then I realised that I had surfaced again, and immediately resumed the fight to hold on to existence. The logs, human bodies – alive and dead, and all the pitiful wreckage tossed helplessly in the fading light. New hope came to me when I reached a thick baulk of timber that did not spin too rapidly as long as I kept still.

The destroyers were standing quite a long way off, and could not move in to pick up survivors, for by now oil covered the water, and there was a risk of igniting it. Knowing this, men still called hoarsely for help. I manoeuvred myself towards a log that had about half a dozen men holding on to it, and by steadying both logs, we were all able to have some rest. In the dim light I could see that the men were in poor shape and covered in black shiny oil, through which their eyes gleamed. One man had his arm around the waist of a man who was in the water. He was clearly dead, and we reasoned with the man to let him go. We had to force him for his own good to release his hold, and in the struggle we were thrown off both logs. Again I had to search feverishly for something to hold on to. While under the surface, I felt my feet against something solid, and gave a heave upwards, which brought me to the surface alongside a log that I grabbed. Then came the thought that haunts me to this day, was that solid object a man who was surfacing, and had been thrust back down by me using his body as a leverage? Did I steal his life?

I lay on the log weary and spent. Now I had given up all hope of rescue. I was too weak to struggle, and all my thoughts were of sleep. I laid my head on my arms, feeling every lap of water enter and leave my mouth. It was then that unconsciousness enveloped my tired body.

When my eyes opened, it was to see suede shoes and grey flannels. I was lying on the floor of a small room and from a long way off a man's voice said, "Hello. You've come round. I'm the M.O. and you're on a destroyer making for the shore. We should reach harbour about two o'clock." I later realised that I had been in the water for 18 hours.

I could not speak or move, although my craving for water forced me to croak unintelligibly but persistently. The officer looked at me with concern and departed abruptly. He returned in a short time and obligingly handed me a bedpan, looking quite baffled when I feebly tried to shake my head. I must have slept again for when I awoke another man was there. He must have realised my terrible thirst and fetched a cup of water. Once again came disappointment, for he did not lift my head, and drinking water flat on one's back is an almost impossible feat. I later had recurring dreams of buying a thermos flask full of ice-cold water so that I would never be thirsty again!

My memories of being carried on a stretcher from the ship are blurred. There seemed to be crowds of civilians on the quay, and I seem to remember a woman sobbing as she peered closely at me perhaps searching for a familiar face that might lie beneath the oil and grime. There followed many weeks in hospital, where I read a newspaper with the heading "Additional survivors of H.M.S. *Courageous.*" There followed three names – the last one was L. A. Collins. I still have that paper, as a reminder of names that were not on the list. Names of my comrades, unsung heroes who were themselves worthy of the proud name of their ship, in the way that they lived and died with the aircraft carrier *Courageous.*

The official communiqué stated:

> *On 17th September 1939, Kapitänleutnant Otto Schubert in the type VII U boat U29, torpedoed and sank HMS Courageous in the South-West approaches (S.W. Ireland) 159nm WSW of Mizen Head, Ireland. The carrier went down in only twenty minutes and 518 of her 1,200 complement went with her, including her commander, Captain W. T. Makeig-Jones.*

Leonard Collins was eventually discharged from the RAF on the 7th July 1940, as being "Below Air Force physical standard."

*The sinking of the aircraft carrier HMS Courageous.
Crew members can be seen in the water.*

Bob's Story

Bob Lucas joined the Royal Engineers in 1939. He was assigned to the Bomb Disposal Squad. He was based in Southern Command, and would go to any town in the area that had been bombed. The men would have to dig down until they reached an unexploded bomb and then the Bomb Disposal Officer would take over. He would relate every move he made on a telephone, so that if the bomb exploded, his colleagues would know what stage he had reached in disarming the bomb. When in Southampton, the men loaded a bomb onto a lorry after its fuse had been removed, however the crew were unaware that a second fuse existed – it was a magnetic fuse and activated in contact with the lorry. Some of Bob's squad were killed in the explosion. After this incident all Bomb Disposal vehicles had a thick rubber mat fitted in the load-carrying area. Later, visiting a soap works that had been bombed, there was another explosion killing three of the squad, but Bob and nine others survived. They were sent to a military hospital in Netley, on Southampton Water – a hospital so large that it had its own dock. Soldiers who had been discharged from the hospital wore a black ribbon on their shoulder epaulet to indicate their discharge from military service on medical grounds. Bob, who had received blast injuries to his eyes, was downgraded from A1 to A3, and was transferred to the Pioneer Corps.

Bob now went to Godshill, in the New Forest, where the War Office was testing techniques in dealing with bombs. Scientists there would bury bombs, and then drill holes, setting up equipment to check the vibrations. On his arrival the Sergeant Major said, "I've got a job for you. You're going to be a batman!" Bob was not impressed. However, Major Abercrombie wasn't too demanding – as long as Bob kept him supplied with whisky, he was happy. Bob would take sugar from the cookhouse to barter with the barmaids of the many public houses in the area.

Then Bob was moved to Warminster helping to build Boreham camp. During one leave, Bob met Glenis Grove in a dance in Penclawdd, and stayed in touch with her. En route to camp, Bob left his kit with an Artillery sergeant – known to Bob as Sergeant Quack – on a railway station, while he went for a drink with some Swansea lads. When he returned to the station, everything had gone! Sergeant, kit and rifle! A Redcap arrested Bob. Now, while he awaited his court martial, Bob had plenty of free time to write to Glenis. On the advice of a friend, Bob challenged the court proceedings, stating that defending and prosecuting officers had discussed his case in the Officers' Mess. The charges were reluctantly wiped out, the officer in charge describing Bob as "a barrack room lawyer."

Bob eventually recovered his kit from Exeter, and was sent to Bletchley Park, where academics were attempting to crack the Enigma code. Bob had to sign the Official Secrets Act, and whilst in Bletchley was given a cigar by the American Ambassador, Wendall Wilkie. Bob and some friends were encouraged to sing in a local pub, but the authorities in Bletchley felt that by doing this they had become a security risk. Their argument was – if a man could be coaxed to sing, he could be coaxed to talk! Commander Travers, the officer in charge of Bletchley, told them, "We don't want buskers here! I don't expect that you will return from your next assignment!" Next morning they were away!

Bob joined a Forward Bridging Unit in a holding camp in Plumpton racecourse. He joined '5 Agra', – their emblem was a Flying Boar. The men were taken by lorries to Newhaven, and sailed in the D Day convoys. Bob remembers that there were ships as far as the eye could see, and they spent all day landing the men on the beaches. Bob was fortunate that his boat landed on the sand as some men had to wade chest deep through the water towards the shore. The men spent the night on the beach, later taking shelter in a nearby quarry. A Beachmaster controlled all the troop movements. The British sent up balloons to deter planes that were strafing the men on the beaches. Bob's team was now responsible for building bridges, each man having his assigned task under the control of the Bridgemaster. The men received double rations, as their work was physically very demanding – a large rum ration was also included. His squad was responsible for building the second longest Bailey bridge of the Second World War – across the river Waal, on what

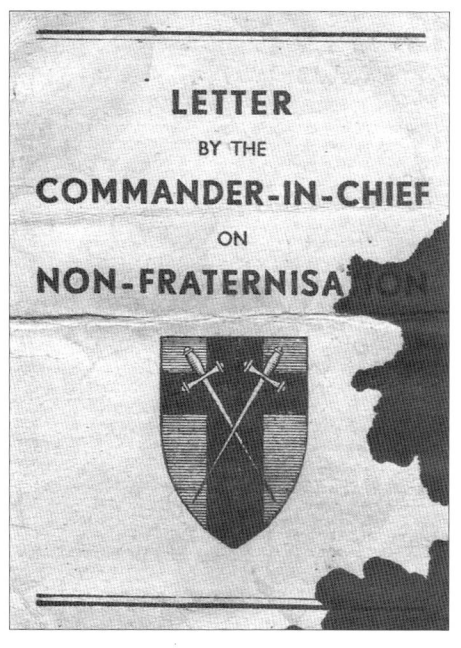

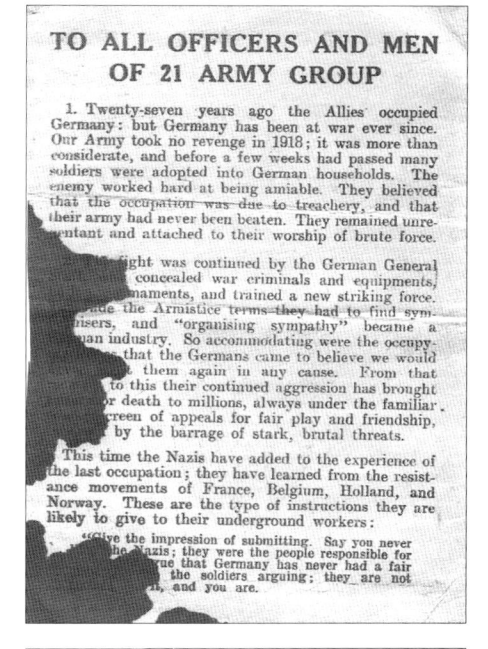

LETTER BY THE COMMANDER-IN-CHIEF ON NON-FRATERNISATION

TO ALL OFFICERS AND MEN OF 21 ARMY GROUP

1. Twenty-seven years ago the Allies occupied Germany: but Germany has been at war ever since. Our Army took no revenge in 1918; it was more than considerate, and before a few weeks had passed many soldiers were adopted into German households. The enemy worked hard at being amiable. They believed that the occupation was due to treachery, and that their army had never been beaten. They remained unrepentant and attached to their worship of brute force.

[The f]ight was continued by the German General [Staff who] concealed war criminals and equipments, [arm]aments, and trained a new striking force. [They eva]ded the Armistice terms; they had to find sym[pathi]sers, and "organising sympathy" became a [Germ]an industry. So accommodating were the occupy[ing powers] that the Germans came to believe we would [not fight] them again in any cause. From that [day] to this their continued aggression has brought [war or] death to millions, always under the familiar [sc]reen of appeals for fair play and friendship, [backed] by the barrage of stark, brutal threats.

This time the Nazis have added to the experience of the last occupation; they have learned from the resistance movements of France, Belgium, Holland, and Norway. These are the type of instructions they are likely to give to their underground workers:

"Give the impression of submitting. Say you never [liked] the Nazis; they were the people responsible for [war]. Argue that Germany has never had a fair [deal. Get] the soldiers arguing; they are not [Nazis], and you are.

"Use old folks, girls, and children, and 'play up' every case of devastation or poverty. Ask the troops to your homes; sabotage or steal equipment, petrol or rations. Get troops to sell these things, if you can. Spread stories about Americans and Russians in the British zone, and about the British to other Allies."

3. Because of these facts, I want every soldier to be clear about "non-fraternisation". Peace does not exist merely because of a surrender. The Nazi influence penetrates everywhere, even into children's schools and churches. Our occupation of Germany is an act of war of which the first object is to destroy the Nazi system. There are Allied organisations whose work it is to single out, separate and destroy the dangerous elements in German life. It is too soon for you to distinguish between "good" and "bad" Germans: you have a positive part to play in winning the peace by a code of behaviour. In streets, houses, cafes, etc., you must keep clear of Germans, man, [woman] and child, unless you meet them in the course of duty. You must not walk out with them, or shake hands, visit their homes, or make them gifts, or take [gifts] from them. You must not play games with [them or] share any social event with them. In short, you [must] not fraternise with Germans at all.

4. To refrain from fraternisation is not easy. [It] requires self-discipline. But in Germany you will have to remember that laughing and eating and dancing with Germans would be bitterly resented by your o[wn] families, by millions of people who have suffered un[der] the Gestapo and under the Luftwaffe's bom[bs and] every Ally that Britain possesses. You [must] remember that these are the same Germ[ans who,] a short while ago, were drunk with victory, [loudly] boasting what they as the Master Race [would do with] you as their slaves, who were applaud[ing the]

disregard by their leaders of any form of decency or of honourable dealings: the same Germans whose brothers, sons and fathers were carrying out a system of mass murder and torture of defenceless civilians. You will have to remember that these same Germans are planning to make fools of you again and to escape the loathing which their actions deserve.

5. Our consciences are clear; "non-fraternisation" to us implies no revenge; we have no theory of master races. But a guilty nation must not only be convicted: it must realise its guilt. Only then can the first steps be taken to re-educate it, and bring it back into the society of decent humanity.

[Ger]man discipline, though not our sort, is [good]. The people will judge you with no amateur [eye, a]nd any slackness will be the cue for the [res]istance movements to intensify their efforts.

[B]e just; be firm; be correct; give orders, and [not arg]ue. Last time we won the war and let the [peace] out of our hands. This time we must not [fail –] we must win both the war and the peace.

B. L. Montgomery
Field-Marshal,
C-in-C 21 Army Group.

Non-fraternisation instructions to the soldiers.

remained of a railway bridge that had been destroyed by the retreating Germans. Bob travelled through Belgium and Holland – where the Dutch people were so hungry that they were reduced to eating their pets and flower bulbs. When crossing the Rhine by boat, the British fired tracer shells low over the river to help the boats keep in their lanes to the landing areas or risk destruction. Although Bob recalled that ferrying the troops across the Rhine was difficult and stressful, it was equally stressful to try and prevent people from using the empty returning boats as an opportunity to flee from Germany.

Bob and his company arrived in Belsen a few days after it had been liberated, and he will never forget the tragic sights that met him there. He was based at Lüneburg where the trials of those in charge of Belsen were being held. The accused were paraded through the streets on their way to their trials.

When Bob was in Lüneburg, the war came to an end, and Montgomery signed the Treaty opposite the camp where Bob was based.

Brenda Jones was in the RAF, based in airfields at various locations, including Innsworth, Glos., Holmsley South and Down Ampney.

Daisy Williams was in the ATS in Bagshot.

WORLD WAR II

Dora Jones, back row, 2nd from right, worked in a Munitions factory on The Point, Penclawdd.

Ivy Griffiths recalls . . .
During the war, I helped my father, G. I. Thomas, run his haulage business, as my two brothers had gone to war, sadly not to return. I was strong enough to do long work hours driving the lorries – delivering various commodities to farms, and carrying coal and hay. At one time I drove the rubbish lorry, and did waste collections in Bishopston. I had a smart uniform with trousers – seldom worn by women in those days – and also drove the post delivery van, cycling to Reynoldston daily to pick the van up.

Gower Church Magazine, February 1945 . . .
Burials. Mrs. Bourne, daughter of late Mr. and Mrs. Gordon, Weobley Farm, at Shanghai, where she had been interned by the Japanese. She had a fine record of thirty years service as a missionary in China. Her husband too, had served in China for an equal number of years, and we extend to him our very sincere sympathy in his great loss. Two brothers Mr. C. Gordon, and Mr. T. Gordon and a sister Mrs. Beynon survive.

Mrs. Avis Marshall recalls her aunt, Mrs. Bourne . . .
My aunt was a missionary in China for thirty years; returning to Weobley Castle on furlough, with presents of parasols and Shantung silk. Her husband was also a missionary, and during the war they were interned in Shanghai. Mrs. Bourne died in a Japanese prisoner-of-war camp there, and her ashes were brought home for burial in Llanrhidian churchyard.

Oswald's Story
by Jeremy Griffiths

At the age of 19 years, Oswald Griffiths was called up for the army and was sent as part of the British Expeditionary Force to France. Victory was snatched from the jaws of defeat at Dunkirk, and the heroic evacuation brought Oswald back to these shores only to be dispatched to North Africa. The Seventh Army massed in readiness for Montgomery's attack on Rommel, and the supply lines for Tripoli were well known to Ossy. The enemy did not put a mark on him – but a British army captain insisted on driving one day, and then proceeded to turn the vehicle over. Ossy was returned to Devizes, England, for many months of medical care. It transpired that the captain had never driven before.

Once fit for duty again, Ossy was sent to Southern Italy, especially Naples, for the southern push up into Germany. He saw very bloody fighting, especially at Monte Casino.

Leonard Jones (The Common, Llanrhidian)

Leonard Jones, 2nd from right.

During the Second World War, Leonard, who was in the army was sent to Italy. Whilst there, he was badly injured in the jaw by a shell, and was left lying in No Man's Land for many hours, until he was brought back to safety by a Ghurkha soldier. Leonard was eventually repatriated to Wales, and spent many months in hospital in Chepstow, having several operations of reconstructive surgery.

Frank Jones (Harewoods, Llanrhidian)
by Glenda Gordon

In 1942, Frank Jones joined the Royal Welsh Fusiliers. Around D Day, 1944, when Frank and his comrades were clearing the woods around Caen, they came under intensive fire. Most of his comrades were killed, and Frank was badly wounded in the back and legs. He was flown back

Frank Jones.

to Stockton-upon-Tees to undergo operations. He was eventually transferred to Morriston Hospital, and later to Llwyn Derw to convalesce. Frank died at the young age of forty from the injuries he sustained during the war.

Frank during his stay in hospital.

A collection of some of the poignant cards sent to his family in Llanrhidian during World War I by Parry Williams (Baytree House). One, dated Christmas 1916, reads:
"Wishing you all a Merry Christmas and a Happy New Year, your loving son, Parry."
Another (overleaf), is heavily scored by the censor's pencil.

TO MY DEAR MOTHER

From your loving Son

Love and Kisses

POST CARD   POSTKAART

CORRESPONDANCE

Parry's Cross, 1908.
The boy taking the geese to the marsh is Ivor Parry, and Mary Jackson Rose Cottage (now Riverside) walks towards Parry's Cross.
(Photograph by kind permission of Dick and Edna Beynon).

George Thomas's membership certificate for the Oddfellows Society, signed in 1908 by Glyn Grove.

Sampler made by Mary Jenkins, aged 11, in 1903. She was the mother of Nancy and Emrys Dunn.

GOWER DAVIES
by Eileen Hutin

During the war, my uncle Gower Davies sent a letter home to his family saying that he had heard from Auntie Martha. This surprised them, as she had died years before the war began. Then they realised that this was his way of telling them where he was, as Aunt Martha's surname was Holland!

Gower Davies was injured in the war, and was flown home. He was nursed in Morriston Hospital, where every soldier was issued with a blue suit and red tie to wear if they were well enough to go outside the hospital, so that they would be recognised as soldiers.

JOHN HUTIN
by Eileen Hutin

John lied about his age so that he could join the RAF in the Second World War. His dream was to be a pilot, and he went to Oxford to take the exams. there, and passed them all. Unfortunately, in spite of this, he failed a crucial test – he was too short in the leg! So John joined the Royal Navy. He served with the rank of Able Seaman, as a RN personnel on a merchant ship under a scheme called DEMS – Defensively

John Hutin.

Equipped Merchant Ships. His ship made many trips to Argentina, travelling up the River Plate to Rio de Janeiro, and when on shore the RN personnel had to wear civilian dress.

In one city, John and some colleagues were arrested and put into gaol, until John, attempting to explain who they were, said "mariners". This word was recognised, and they were set free.

John travelled extensively during the war, visiting Burma and India as well as South America. Finally, John joined a ship and in great secrecy the men were issued with khaki shirts and shorts, but had no idea where they were sailing. There was an announcement one day on the loudspeaker that said that the atomic bomb had been dropped on Hiroshima. The ship turned about and the war was over!

HOME DEFENCE

Gower Church Magazine, 1941. Parish of Llanrhidian . . .
On June 26th, various branches of the Gower AFS held a very successful gathering at the church hall, where certificates were presented to various members by Councillor Digby Jones. A dance held in the hall terminated a very happy evening.

WORLD WAR II

*Sidney Williams receives his certificate from Councillor Digby Jones.
Included in this photograph are: Councillors Glyn Grove and Stanley John,
Tom Tucker, Fred Morris, Phil Grove, Will Morgan and Cyril Jeffreys.*

*AFS Llanrhidian.
Included here are: Dai Gronow, Will Morgan, Glanmor Williams, Dai Davies, Richie Shepherd,
Aneuren Gordon, Cyril Jeffreys and Glyn Mabbett.*

Llanrhidian Home Guard, Moormills.
Back row: Elvet Jeffreys, Allen Gwyn, Frederick Jones, Arthur Jones, Major Williams, Stanley Willis, Leslie Williams, John Williams, and Jack Harry.
Centre: Bert Morris, Gwynfor Davies, Alan Grove, Ronald Jones, Harold Jones, Stanley Jones, Elwyn John, Dennis Jeffreys and Ronald Morgan.
Front row: Stanley Dunn, William Beynon, Glyn Grove, Ronald Winch, George Roberts, Haydn Williams, Reggie Morris and David Jones.

World War II in the Church Hall
Remembered by Eileen Hutin

During the war, soldiers from two regiments were billeted in the Church Hall – the Royal Sussex and the Black Watch. As there were no washing facilities in the hall, two soldiers each night would visit local homes that had a bathroom, for a bath and a simple supper of bread and cheese or jam.

Every night, two soldiers would arrive at my parents' home, Hillcrest, for their baths. One soldier from this time has kept in touch with us. He is Charlie Hicks from London and we still get a calendar from him every Christmas. When the soldiers moved to Reynoldston he still walked over to Hillcrest to ask, "What's for supper?" Another soldier, Charlie Hill, was a wonderful pianist, and would play the piano in the parlour after his bath and supper. We heard later that many of these soldiers did not survive the D Day invasion.

WARTIME STORIES

Eleanor Froom . . .
After the Three Nights' Blitz of Swansea, my uncle, George Thomas, came to take me back to Llanrhidian in his lorry, but he had to leave it in Waunarlwydd because of the bomb craters in the roads. "Thy'll sleep tonight, maid," he told me – but I didn't. That night they dropped a stick of bombs on Welsh Moor, killing six or seven cattle there.

Thelma Pritchard . . .
The comedian Frankie Howerd was stationed in Penclawdd, and gave many concerts in the church hall in Llanrhidian. He became friendly with the villagers here, especially my parents, Kenny and Patty Williams, Bay Tree House, where he often ate a hearty lunch.

Janie Hutin . . .
The aerodrome was built on Fairwood Common during the war. To confuse the enemy planes, a decoy aerodrome was put on Cefn Bryn, alongside the road. It was just a few lights, and Mr. Rees Shepherd, New Parks, was the night watchman there. We also had 'Gertie' – a frame of flashing lights – near the Greyhound at Oldwalls. It would give signals during the night.

Dick Beynon . . .
George Davies, The Dolphin, known to everyone in Llanrhidian as 'Doctor', would give a free pint and a packet of Players cigarettes to every soldier home on leave.

Audrey Williams . . .
I remember walking through St. Mary's, Swansea some time after the Three Nights' Blitz, and seeing the upturned clock face from St. Mary's Church lying on the ground with the hands stopped at twenty to eleven.

Janie Hutin remembers . . .
During the 1939-45 War, American soldiers were billeted in Penclawdd and surrounding areas. Before D Day, some of the American soldiers trained on Cefn Bryn. All the farmers around the hill were given pieces of metal shaped like triangles and painted yellow, which they had to nail around the farmhouse, garden, outbuildings and yard. The soldiers were not to come inside these signs. It was very strange to see so much traffic and men on Cefn Bryn, especially in March. They would drive

their jeeps up and down, the soldiers marching and completely covered in bracken. All one could see was the fern moving about. They had to dig trenches to sleep in at night. It went very cold with a hard frost during the time they were there, and sadly some died from the cold, as they had dug their trenches in the wetter parts. Whilst there, they had to live on their rations and a can of water. But they would stop the baker from Reynoldston on his rounds to buy bread.

The soldiers had been warned on no account to drink any water off the hill, although we, like everyone else on the Bryn, had always fetched our water from the wells there. One evening, a sergeant came to our farm and asked my father if some of his soldiers could sleep in our sheds. Dad was quite willing, as long as they put out their cigarettes, which they did readily. At that time, there were four cattle tied to one side of the shed, so the soldiers slept on the other side, the remainder sleeping alongside our hay and straw ricks in the rickyard. The sergeant brought about six soldiers into the house to sleep. They made us soup and drinking chocolate from their dried packets, things we didn't see at that time.

My grandfather, father, mother, sister and myself went upstairs to bed, leaving them with a good fire and an oil lamp on the table. When we got up, they had all returned to their trenches on the hill. A few days later, the hill was empty again, they had all returned to their billets ready for D Day. We found out later that most of them had lost their lives during the invasion.

When we knew that the 'Yanks' were going to be training around us, there were a number of gruesome rumours about – that they would be horrible, nasty people with knives, and no one would be safe. We went to bed, left them in the house and buildings. They were human beings like everyone, young men, miles from their country and glad of any little home comforts.

Schoolboy Memories

Donald Lewis and Roger Jones were young lads when World War II began. Here are their memories.

Donald Lewis, Weobley Castle . . .
In the summer holidays of 1942, I was playing with Dennis Hughes, whose father owned Windmill Farm, which was just across the road from where I lived in Weobley Castle. We were playing at the back of the house at the end of their garden, when we heard the familiar sound of the aeroplanes and the rat-a-tat of machine gun fire.

WORLD WAR II

I hope you are keeping well, because it has been very cold down in Llanidan this month.

We have not got a pig this year but mama is thinking to have one if we can get plenty of food for it.

One day when it was wet and dad could not go to work, mama sent dad down to shop to get a pot of paint for; dad to paint the boards outside the box room.

When John and Dennis William were walking down by the hall, they were challenged by a sentry, who told them to come to him to get recognised, and when they got to the sentry he told them to get out of the way.

On thursday nights a lot of insendery bombs droped (↓) down in cwmwy farm yard, and they droped in hedges down Llanmadoc one landed in mrs Jefreys the shops garden and very nearly lite the shop up, Then the plane came up along the coast to Llanelthy and just before it ~~got~~ there was a big exploshion and a lot of lights hung down in a row, all the surchlights went down, and there was no sound of a plane, so we think it was shot down.

Mama will becoming to see you (soon) soon.

Love from Wilfred.

"To Grandpa, love from Wilfred." A letter written by Wilfred Grove, aged 9, during the Second World War.

Cynthia Jones and the Home Guard at the Sawmills, Cillibion.

Then we knew this was the usual 'Whirlwind fighters' having target practice on the eastern side of Cefn Bryn. After a few minutes, we again heard a rat-a-tat, but this time accompanied by the whirl of bullets, so we hid behind a tree, then there was a thump and about two yards in front of us this hole in the ground appeared. It entered at a shallow angle about a foot long, and about three inches deep. Digging down with our pocket-knives we dug out this 20mm cannon shell, shiny and hot.

So we boys were the proud owners of a recently fired bullet. I still can't remember who kept it. This firing practice was eventually stopped after the RAF was shown the bullet; they thought people had been complaining about the empty shell cases that were falling. After this, the only casualty was a gander from Windmill Farm.

Roger Jones, Cillibion, writes . . .
The day before we moved to Cillibion, General Eisenhower reviewed the US troops in Gower, and all their army lorries had been parked one behind the other from Cillibion all the way to Reynoldston, in preparation for Eisenhower to take the salute. I remember that the following day the troops moved out of Gower in readiness for D Day. Some of the jeeps around our house were decorated with branches of lilac that the soldiers had picked from our hedge.

The Black Watch Regiment also carried out manoeuvres on Cefn Bryn.

I well remember one day, soldiers came running down from Welshmoor, taking cover, firing, and then running again. One soldier, complete with his Black Watch cap, used our chestnut tree as cover. Coloured smoke, bangs and mortar explosions accompanied these manoeuvres, after which I would often find mortar cases, and frequently ·303 blanks.

A Small Boy and a Big War

I had my tenth birthday in the week that the Second World War broke out. I have always been glad that I was of an age that I could follow all the news in the papers, and on the wireless, over the whole period of one of the great events of history, perhaps the greatest of the twentieth century.

Living in the heart of the country, and in south west Wales, very distant from the mainland of Europe, one would not expect many direct effects of the war – that is apart from things which affected everyone, like rationing of food, and clothing, shortages of almost every commodity

Eric Morgan with his brother Ronald's Home Guard rifle.

from footballs to paper. However, if you wanted lipsticks, watches or fountain pens, Willie Davies, the Post Office, could probably get you one. What a character he was and a yarn spinner. His bad experience of being gassed in World War One was far behind him.

Other common experiences were the carrying of gas masks, the evacuation of children, the blackout, and seeing a multiplicity of uniforms. Two notable absences were signposts and the ringing of church bells, the ringing of which would signify an invasion. The big local indication of preparations against invasion was the erection of thousands of timber posts over the six miles of the southern 'Gower' side of the Burry estuary. It was reckoned that the huge flat area of hard muddy sand would be suitable for landing aircraft. Indeed, the American aeronaut Amelia Earhart had famously landed there in the 1930s. The calmer, shallower waters at high tide could certainly favour landing craft coming from the sea. Later in the War, British, Canadian and American troops practised landings on the Gower coast, using various craft including 'ducks' – the nickname for DUKWs (whatever these initials stood for!).

The nature of the muddy sand was a factor in bringing to Crofty (Pencaerfenni Point), a branch of artillery proofing range from Shoeburyness on the Thames estuary. At this 'experimental establishment', which we called 'The Point', firing ranges were built and the shells recovered at low tide. It was said that when some particularly important new ammunition was being tested, Prime Minister Churchill had been known to phone directly for information about results. We lived with this artillery noise throughout the war, but the biggest weapons, large calibre naval guns, were fired at long range from Berthlwyd, an area where even fewer people lived. Crofty village suffered the most noise, and many cracked windowpanes, as a result of the vibration from the firing.

The first plane crash in Gower actually happened just before the war began, when an Avro Anson narrowly failed to clear Rhossili Downs, in bad visibility. All the crew were killed. We walked up to see the wreckage, and my brother Ronald picked up a bit to bring home. It was partly of wood. I was amazed how much wood seemed to be in the construction. Other crashes I particularly remember were, naturally, in Llanrhidian. A Tomahawk came down near Manselfold, but the other crash I saw happen. I was delivering Sunday papers and, when at Newton Farm, saw several Spitfires doing exercises at fairly low level. One lost control and spiralled down to crash near Tom Pearce's, a hundred yards or so from Broad Pool. The pilot turned out to be a nineteen-year-old Canadian.

Not far from there, on the upper part of Cefn Bryn, Whirlwind ground attack light bombers practised machine-gunning for a time. Farmers well to the west of the Bryn complained that stray bullets could sometimes be heard whistling by. A little adventure for boys, like my cousin Wilfred Grove and myself, was to comb the heather for brass shell casings, which made very smart candlesticks. We also collected tail fins in the area behind Llanrhidian Common. These were from incendiary bombs dropped by mistake or by jettisoning from German bombers. High explosive bombs also fell here and there, for example at Cillibion Farmhouse a large unexploded bomb was found in the orchard, and was later blown up on Cefn Bryn. Three craters on Welsh Moor can still be seen, but the most interesting crater was quickly filled in. It was caused by one of the first bombs (along with some in the Orkney Isles) to be dropped in Britain. It fell in the road at Llanmorlais in July 1940, and children who were on their way to school to sit their CWB examination were unable to get through, and had to sit their exam. later. Another bomb fell nearby in the same raid, and there was a loss of life – a pig was killed!

I only saw one German aircraft for certain, and that was at very high altitude, but I recognised it because of its distinctive shape. It was a Kondor, then the largest bomber in the world. I saw several aircraft caught in searchlight, and presume that they were German, but as silvery specks I could not identify them. One German aircraft did not escape.

It exploded over the estuary with shattering flashes and made an indelible impression on us. We'd shot a Jerry down! I don't remember anyone remarking on the men on board. I also remember walking with a group of lads along the road approaching Hillcrest, when one of us made an idle remark and got a response out of the darkness. A platoon of American infantry, faces blackened, was hunched into the batter (bank) alongside the road.

Quite early in the war, troops were stationed all over Gower, and billeted in village halls. First in Llanrhidian were the Royal Sussex Regiment and others followed including the Black Watch who had just returned from Iceland and had polar bear shoulder flashes.

Our local men undertook part-time war duties. Glyn Grove and Kenny Williams were air raid wardens. A very specialist duty was 'decontamination' in case of gas. Byron Tucker was one of these. Brynley Jones was the leading fireman in the village and the firemen kept night duty sleeping in the clubroom upstairs in the Welcome to Town. Their equipment at first consisted of a large hand pump, but they eventually were equipped with a better machine, and actually put a fire out on one occasion – not caused by enemy action!

The largest number of men involved in voluntary duties was in the Home Guard. George Roberts of the Greyhound Inn was appointed Sergeant, because he had once belonged to the Gower Yeomanry, but the effective leader was Dai Jones, Uplands, who was a Corporal. My brother Ronald was made a Lance corporal, and like the other members of the squad had a rifle. It was a very old model, but I loved to help him clean it. Shooting practice took place at Moormills near Cae Forgan. On one occasion, an exercise was arranged in which Llanmadoc Home Guard were to attack Llanrhidian. A couple of us teenagers thought that our Home Guard didn't seem to be organised, so we went off on our own to try to locate them, and found them going along the hedge at Llwyn y bwch and reported back. The Llanmadoc men were not pleased about this and shouted at us after their 'capture'. I can remember Mr. O'Sullivan quite red in the face.

National registration numbers were allotted to every person following an abnormal census. (The official 1941 census was never held.) My father was the local enumerator. Each district was coded with four letters and each family in it with a number; family members were then numbered in sequence. As the fifth in my family, my number was XLFB 92:5. These numbers were used by the new National Health Service after the war, and for other purposes for many years afterwards.

Social life flourished in these years of deprivation and tension. The

Women's Institute, Comforts Fund, and Home Guard organised dances, whist drives and concerts. Outdoor events using tents were not held. The women organised tea and refreshments as best they could considering the rationing. This was for the band and servicemen particularly. I remember on one occasion in the church hall, my mother in her pinny was standing in the doorway to the kitchen near to the stage, when a youthful Frankie Howerd dragged her up on the stage to assist in his act. I was standing at the back, very uneasy and blushing. Frankie was a private and on Sundays we would see him on his way from The Point where he was stationed to Llanrhidian Church. We were amused to see him wearing brown kid gloves.

At last – VE Day! The war was over. We could pull down the black out curtains, peel the brown sticky strips of paper off our windows – and celebrate. That night we had a bonfire, mostly old tyres bare of tread and everyone gathered round. All the kids were on the village green. One of the boys got tight, or pretended to, on numerous bottles of cider pop. We fitted a bulb in our outside light and then remembered the old WWI searchlight mirror we had been given by George Jones, The Prisk. My brother, on leave, took a couple of leads and fitted big bulbs into the other ends. By placing them at the right point in front of the huge concave mirror, he created a searchlight good enough to illuminate Nant y Wrach about 500 yards away. In earlier years, my brother and his Home Guard friend Reggie Morris thought they were very daring to send Morse code messages by flashing torchlights between The Common and Stavel Hagar. 'Put that light out!' was one of the famous wartime cries, like the slogan 'Dig for Victory' or the song title 'There'll always be an England'.

Hiroshima and VJ Day followed soon. The world couldn't count the dead or measure the suffering, but no one dared this time to say, "the war to end all wars."

Llanrhidian deaths began very early with Arthur Harry who became seriously ill on active service, and Griff Gwyn of Stonyford. Few mothers can have suffered more than Mrs. Thomas of Mount Pleasant Farm whose two sons were killed, and Frank and Leonard Jones were both badly wounded, while Ernie Grove was taken prisoner in Crete.

In a strange way we were all victims, and all hurt, but survived into a new world. The village and village life recovered and carried on . . . to continue its history, a history worth remembering and recording.

To use another wartime saying, I feel I have now 'done my bit'.

Eric Morgan

The Evacuees

Many children from London and Kent were evacuated to Gower in 1940, when a German invasion of Britain seemed imminent. The school register for the time records that 119 children came to the North Gower villages, the majority staying with families in Llanrhidian. Two teachers accompanied the children, and a school was opened for them in the vestry of Ebenezer Chapel, Oldwalls. Amongst the children who stayed with families in the village were Lottie May who stayed at The Mill, with Mr. and Mrs. Stanley Willis, Pat Green who stayed at Baytree with Kenny and Patty Williams, and Marjorie Davies who stayed with the Williams family, Pant Glas, and her brother John who was with Mrs. Shepherd, New Parks. Many of the children returned home in 1941, but have stayed in touch with the families who cared for them. One evacuee, John Lionel Kemp, still lives in Llanrhidian today.

Jack Kemp's story . . .
I was born in Paddington Green, and, on 7th September 1940 when I was eight years old, my three sisters and I were taken to Paddington Station. There was a full trainload of children there, each with a case, gas mask, sandwiches and a label. We arrived at High Street Station, Swansea, and were taken by buses to Penmaen Workhouse, where we spent our first night. Next day we were taken in groups to different halls in Gower to be allocated to families in the area. I went with Ernest Richards to Bank Farm, Horton, and my sisters went to different families, although as my youngest sister was only 5 years old, my eldest sister went as well to look after her. I was in Bank Farm from September to Christmastime, spending most of my time with Will Beynon of Westonside, helping with the farm animals, especially the calves, but then I contracted ringworm and was sent to Stouthall to recover. I was then sent to Chalks of Rhossili, but would return to see Will Beynon whenever I could, and I asked him if I could stay with him. As this wasn't possible, Will contacted his brothers Daniel and Tom in Llethrid, telling them he knew of a boy who wanted to live on a farm, and in 1941 I went to stay with them in Llethrid.

In 1941, my mother came to Gower to fetch my youngest sister home and eventually all my sisters returned to London. After the war, I returned to London for a short time, and went to Farming College in Lewes, Sussex. At 16, I returned to Llethrid, staying there until I joined the RAF for my National Service. On being invalided out, I returned to Llethrid, and have lived in Gower ever since.

4

Llanrhidian at Work

Stavel Hagar.

THE DIX FAMILY, STAVEL HAGAR (WEAVERS)
Remembered by Peggy Shepherd

My great grandparents, Joseph and Mary Dix, lived in Stavel Hagar. They were woollen weavers, and employed people to work in the factory there. They made a variety of woollen goods, including blankets, shawls and quilts. Part of the loom was above the front door of the farmhouse when I was a child. My great uncle, Richard Dix, was the last of the family connected with weaving, which finished in Llanrhidian in 1904, the year that my father was born. Richard Dix dismantled the looms and went to live in The Rallt, Llanmorlais.

Joseph Dix stayed on in the farmhouse after his son Richard Dix left. Joseph also had three daughters, Polly, Harriet and Margaret. In the Llanrhidian school log book for 1898, Margaret Dix is recorded as the sewing teacher.

My great aunt, Harriet Dix, lived with us until her death in 1950. She was the last surviving member of the Dix family, Stavel Hagar.

Richard and Martha Dix.

Polly, Harriet and Margaret Dix.

Master and Matron of the Workhouse, Penmaen.

RICHARD AND ELIZABETH DUNN
by Eric Morgan

My great grandparents Richard and Elizabeth Dunn were the Master and Matron of the Workhouse in Penmaen. It was known as 'The Union' as it catered for a union of parishes. Their daughter Louisa would ride sidesaddle on her white horse from Leason Farm across Cefn Bryn to visit her parents.

Richard and Elizabeth Dunn retired on the 1st May 1906, having served as Master and Matron for twenty years. The minutes of meetings held by the 'Gower Guardians' for those years show the day-to-day problems they would have had to deal with. (The Guardians were representatives of the local parishes, responsible for overseeing the running of the workhouse.)

Gower Union Minute Books . . .

March 1897. The Medical Officer and the Master to take such steps as are necessary to effect a speedy cure of the filthy condition of six tramps in the tramp ward, and discharge them as soon as possible.

June 1897. The relieving officer was directed to give the Swansea Union paupers resident in this union the extra allowance of relief in Jubilee Week.

Dec. 1897. Proposed that the indoor paupers be allowed the usual Christmas dinner of roast beef, plum pudding and beer.

Jan. 1900. The Master authorised to procure lamps for the hearse at a cost not exceeding 16/-.

There was a complaint that the Guardians were unable to put their horses in the stable, because the room was occupied by straw.
Tenders accepted on the 18th September 1900, include:

> Swansea Old Brewery Co. Ltd. Reynoldston –
>   Beer 20/- for 18 gallons.
> Richard Gordon, Penrhallt, coal – 36/- a ton.
> W. Abraham, Swansea – beef 6d, mutton 7d and kidney suet 4d.

New dietary tables, 1901.
Instead of bread and gruel for breakfast for four days in the week, I suggest as a change, bread and porridge for one morning. Instead of sago pudding for four days, bread pudding be given twice.

*The Gower Guardians photographed outside the Workhouse, Penmaen.
Thomas Clement, Freedown Farm, Llanrhidian, is in the back row, second from left.*
(Photograph provided by Mrs. D. Tucker).

October 1901. The clerk produced information which he had obtained as to the terms of the three nearest training ships for admitting pauper boys.

In 1906, after the resignation of Richard and Elizabeth Dunn, the new Master and Matron were appointed. Mr. and Mrs. Stanley Dunn (Richard and Elizabeth's son and daughter-in-law), became Master and Matron at a salary of £25 per annum each, together with rations, apartments, washing, etc. and it was agreed that their sons be permitted to reside with them.

Gower Church Magazine, 1906 . . .
The Gower Guardians met on Tuesday, and the Chairman moved that the usual Christmas dinner be given the workhouse paupers. He further proposed that the usual supply of beer be also given. The Rev. D. Davies, Mumbles, moved an amendment that no beer be given. He said there were 400 workhouses in the country where no beer was given on Christmas Day. He strongly objected to the proposition. Mr. Richards, Rhossilly, seconded, and said it was through the beer their workhouses, gaols and asylums were being filled.
The Master said that men received a pint and the women half a pint each. It was the same beer as the Guardians had been having with their luncheon.
The original motion was carried by the casting vote of the chairman.

THE WELCOME TO TOWN
Remembered by Beryl Dunn

The Welcome to Town was in my family for many years. My great grandparents, David and Mary Shepherd, are recorded as living there on the 1881 census, and my grandfather, Frank Shepherd, was born in the Welcome in 1878. Upstairs was the lodge room, which was used to hold village functions. Vestry meetings were held there to determine the poor rate, and to decide if villagers would be entitled to parish relief, and later in 1894, the newly formed parish council met there. It was also a meeting place for the Oddfellows, a benevolent society, and during World War II, it was the headquarters for the Auxiliary Fire Service.

Nowadays, whenever you read about the Welcome to Town, it is mentioned that the ghost of a coachman has been seen in the pub. Well, in all the years that my family lived there, we never saw him!

David and Mary Shepherd, The Welcome to Town, Llanrhidian.

LOT 71.

(Coloured *Green* on Plan No. 4).

ALL THAT FREEHOLD FULLY LICENSED FREE PUBLIC HOUSE & PREMISES

known as

THE "WELCOME TO TOWN," LLANRHIDIAN.

Let with other land forming Lots 72 and 74 and parts of Lots 99, 100 and 102, to David Shepherd, on a yearly tenancy, Ladyday entry, at a rent of £34 per annum, of which the sum of £20 will be apportioned to this Lot.

The House contains: Public Kitchen, Cellar, Larder, Back Kitchen, Parlour, Clubroom, and 3 Bedrooms. There is also a 2-Stall Stable, Cowhouse with 5 ties, Cart House, Pigsty and a piece of Garden Ground, the whole comprising about **35 perches.**

1920 sale notice for the Welcome to Town.

The New Road comes to Llanrhidian

In the late 1920s, the track leading from Llanrhidian to Wernffrwd was widened and a new road built. The Opening Ceremony took place outside the Vicarage, Llanrhidian. Included amongst the dignitaries attending were: the surveyor Mr. Jones, Mr. George Taylor of Vanguard Buses, Mr. George the Master of the Workhouse, Penmaen, Mr. Sam Richards, Rhossilli, Mr. Gordon, Mr. Arthur Griffiths (father of Mrs. D. Tucker), Dr. Morton senior, and Mr. Thomas Clement, Llanrhidian.

A rail track to carry construction material has been laid alongside the road.

The Opening Ceremony.
(Photograph provided by Mrs. D. Tucker).

This house had to be demolished to make way for the New Road.
(Photograph provided by Kevin Lloyd).

The New Road at Wernhalog.
(Photograph provided by Kevin Lloyd).

G. I. Thomas with his haywain, a carthorse in the shafts and a chain horse in front. This was his original means of haulage.

G. I. THOMAS
(MOUNT PLEASANT FARM, LLANRHIDIAN)
by J. Griffiths

George Ivor Thomas was a well-known and well-respected Gower man; having been born, bred, lived and died in Mount Pleasant Farm, Llanrhidian. George was especially known for the family business: 'Geo. I. Thomas', Agricultural Haulage and Hay Merchant. The important parts of his life were his family, business, and the Church, all contained within the community of the village and village life. He was held in high admiration by all who knew him, and was affectionately known as 'Uncle George' to many of all ages.

Both his father, and grandfather before him had been born, lived and died in the same house in Llanrhidian, and are buried with their wives in the family grave in Llanrhidian churchyard.

George and his twin brother John (later known as Jack) were the youngest children of William and Eleanor Thomas, and weighed approx. 11lbs. each at birth on the 23rd Sept. 1890. George married Annie Maria Jeffreys in Cheriton Church on Sunday, 18th November 1913, at 8 a.m.

In the early days of George's working life, he stabled up to three pairs of shire horses for all types of work from farm ploughing locally to hay delivery in Swansea. The shire horses, Daisy and Jessie, were his last – the gentle giants were very much missed. The Cart Shed that was adjacent

George and Jack Thomas.

to the stable was used to house an array of carts for various work purposes. He was an early bird ensuring that the horses were properly turned out for the day's work – polishing leather and brass and grooming the horses. Quarrying stone, cutting rush, operating the local Lime Kiln on Llanrhidian hill, coal deliveries, and last but not least, the market gardening aspect kept the Saturday market stall in Swansea going – and kept the whole family very busy. In addition, George always made time to cut, maintain the upkeep and to remove the grass from the Churchyard for many years. Although very busy all week, George would not work on a Sunday except for feeding the animals.

His Saturdays were Market Days and he would meet up with his brother Jack in Swansea, and in the afternoon he would regularly visit the Empire or the Plaza, returning home with a delicacy for his grand-

> **GEO. IVOR THOMAS,**
> **General Haulier & Hay Merchant,**
> **LLANRHIDIAN, GOWER.**
> TELEPHONE—16 REYNOLDSTON.

Advertisement from the Gower Church Magazine

children – winkles – which they would be fed with relish, with the aid of a pin carried and stored in readiness in his lapel. These trips to Swansea were dual purpose, both business and pleasure. Transporting goods in to Swansea for himself and for the locals, he would also be collecting orders, and essential requirements for the villagers, including supplies for the local shop, which was then sited next door in Mount Pleasant Cottage.

George Thomas enthusiastically embraced the modern innovations of the time and quickly acquired the new-fangled motorised trucks – includ-

G. I. Thomas standing alongside the first lorry in Gower. Will Davies is in the driving seat. This photo was taken in Wassail Square, Swansea.

ing charabanc seating for the back of a lorry for village and church outings. He was one of the first in the area to acquire a telephone and was one of the first car owners too – it was a black Ford, registration no. YJ3038, which was often called upon by the community for hospital runs, weddings, funerals and of course was also used for family outings. Many locals learnt to drive with him on the lorries, including Jim Brockie, Bert Morris, and Cyril Jeffreys, and even more either worked for him or helped with village festivities. A lorry was all-important for the carnivals – collecting chairs, food and erecting and storing the church tent – this being a very important job as it had to be done when it was dry – even the haymaking had to wait for this!

Entertainment was what you made yourself locally, and George was often in the thick of it with his twin brother Jack, including quoits matches, boxing in the stable, the local football team, fancy dress at the Carnival and also competing in the Gower Show in the vegetable section with his prized marrows and pumpkins.

He worked hard and played hard. After a hard day's work he would be encouraged to go to the pub with the lads, which he was happy to do, but he always had a lemonade as he had signed the pledge when he was 16 years of age in 1906 at the Oddfellows Meeting Room at the Welcome to Town.

The deaths of his two sons in the Second World War was an unbearable loss, magnified by the death of his wife on 15th June, 1949, aged 58 years. His daughters, Winnie and Ivy, together with the Church were his rock thereafter. His business being continued by his daughter Ivy and her new husband Ossie – whose decision it was to continue trading as 'G. I. Thomas' – was a joy to George, as were all his grandchildren. But alas further grief was to come with the sudden death of his 14-year-old grandson Julian, on the 15th June 1962 – on the 13th anniversary of his own wife's death.

In later life he enjoyed riding Trigger, the famous white horse of the village, up and down the village to the garage by the school, to save the climb up the hill, and local children would often borrow the horse. Trigger knew who was in charge – he would plod for George and the children, but once the children headed him for home he went much faster.

George and his brother Jack possessed 'twin intuition' knowing instinctively when there was something wrong with the other. In the end, George died aged 75 years on the 9th September 1966, and Jack followed very shortly afterwards on the 3rd December 1966, within 11 weeks of each other.

*Four generations of the Pearce family, Big House, Llanrhidian.
Tom, Will, Thomas and Reg Pearce.*

LLETHRID CHEMICAL WORKS

In a newspaper article of 1933, Tom Pearce, Big House, Llanrhidian, is described as "the oldest man in Gower," and is reported to be 91 years of age. In the interview, Tom recalled his boyhood in Woodbury, near Exeter, and said, "It must have been sixty years or so ago that I came to Gower, where my brother-in-law was bailey-hind to Mr. Bowen, who had a farm and managed Mr. Vivian's chemical works in Llethrid.

I was there 21 years, and you can see the old ruined sheds there still at the side of the road. The produce of this chemical works in Gower was charcoal, naphtha, lime salts, tar and some other products. They were all obtained from timber. Hard timber – the sort that bore berries – was placed in a sealed chamber over fires, with a complicated system of pipes leading from the chamber into water ponds, where the condensation of the gases gave the materials that eventually became naphtha and other products that were used in the Hafod Isa Works.

We used up to 18 tons of timber a week, and we made about 25 gallons of naphtha every week, and the lime salts and charcoal that were used for the refining processes."

When the copper works declined, the works closed.

Reg Pearce (the young boy in the family photograph), recalls the family's connection with Sir Francis Drake . . .

Four generations of my family have received a pension from a fund established by Sir Francis Drake. The first to receive the pension was my great grandfather Tom Pearce, who left Devon in the 1870s and was traced by a solicitor from Exeter. The pension is passed on to the eldest child of the former recipient, but I will be the last to receive the pension as the fund is now closed.

In 1988, as descendants of Sir Francis Drake, my wife Ivy and I were guests at the Armada Ball in Plymouth, celebrating the 400th Anniversary of the Spanish Armada.

THE MILLER OF LLANRHIDIAN

Thomas John Willis, the miller of the Nether Mill, Llanrhidian, is the subject of an article in the *Herald of Wales* on the 23rd January 1932. He is described as the fifth in the generation of the Willis family interested in milling, and the second to work the Llanrhidian mill. Thomas John says his son (Stanley), "is now the one who does the milling, the sixth of the line."

The writer describes the steady clank of the water wheel – at 18 feet the largest in Gower – and watches as oats are crushed, and talks with Thomas John of the miller's hopes that there will be a return to the days where every farmer grew enough corn for his own use – and some over for the market. He continues, "not so long ago Gower-milled wheat could be obtained in Swansea, and there was a restaurant in High Street that specialised in *bara gwenith*, which was bread baked from the wholemeal of Gower."

Ernie Grove remembers . . .
As a boy I remember watching Stanley Willis and his father 'dressing' the millstones. The grooves in the millstone would wear down, and would

*The Willis family, Thomas John, and his wife Elizabeth
with their son, Stanley.*

have to be remade with a hammer and chisel. It was long, tedious work, but the grooves were necessary to hold the grain whilst it was being ground. I found a broken millstone that Thomas John Willis had discarded out on the marsh, and brought it home to make a garden step. Like the millstone outside the Mill, you can clearly see the grooves. That stone had been brought from France.

My friend John Williams and I would wait until Thomas John was having his lunch. Then we would operate! We would ride on the chains that took the grain up to the first floor, often banging our heads on the trap door.

The cogs of the wheel were made of wood, so that the wheel would work quietly. The farmers brought bags of wheat, corn and barley, and

In the High Court of Justice.

CHANCERY DIVISION.   Re DAVIES—DAVIES v. DAVIES.

LLANRHIDIAN, near SWANSEA, GLAMORGANSHIRE

VALUABLE FREEHOLD ESTATE.

PARTICULARS AND CONDITIONS OF SALE

OF A VALUABLE

FREEHOLD
CORN GRIST MILL,

In thorough working order, and very substantially fitted up with the necessary

MACHINERY AND PLANT.

And worked by water, of which there is a plentiful supply; also the

FREEHOLD DWELLING-HOUSE

ADJOINING THE MILL,

Substantially built and in thorough repair, with the GARDEN adjoining,

THE WHOLE SITUATE AND BEING AND KNOWN AS

THE LOWER MILL AND MILL COTTAGE,

Llanrhidian, near Swansea, Glamorganshire,

OF THE ESTIMATED ANNUAL VALUE OF

£30:0:0,

Which will be offered for Sale by Auction,

Pursuant to a Judgment of the Chancery Division of the High Court of Justice made in the above action of *Re* Davies—Davies v. Davies, and with the approbation of His Lordship the MASTER OF THE ROLLS, the Judge to whom the said action is attached,

In ONE LOT, by

MR. CHARLES HUGHES

(Of the Firm of BEYNON & HUGHES),

THE PERSON APPOINTED BY THE JUDGE, AT THE

"WELCOME-TO-TOWN" INN, LLANRHIDIAN,

ON FRIDAY, THE 13TH DAY OF FEBRUARY 1880,

AT THREE O'CLOCK IN THE AFTERNOON,

Particulars and Conditions of Sale may be had of Mr. RICHARD WHITE BEOR, Jun., Solicitor, Swansea; of Mr. O. E. DAWSON, Solicitor, 10 Hart Street, Bloomsbury Square, London, W.C.; and of the Auctioneer,

Mr. CHARLES HUGHES, Victoria Chambers, Oxford Street, Swansea.

Sale notice for Llanrhidian Nether Mill.

would leave them in the Mill. They would return a few days later to pick up the ground corn. There were bags all over the floor waiting to be ground. They were all marked and labelled.

When horse drawn vehicles came down the steep hill towards the Mill, they would use a 'shoe' made of iron that would be put under one wheel holding it still, and acting as a brake. The shoe would be left at the side of the Welcome to be taken up by the returning cart.

The Mill Wheel.

THE NETHER MILL, LLANRHIDIAN
by Elizabeth Thomas, née Willis

There have been mills in Llanrhidian since medieval times, possibly earlier as the community depended on them.

The present building, which dates from 1803, was rebuilt according to the records "at the expense of Wm. Evans, Gent." The masons are recorded as being John Beynon and Evan Jenkin, and the carpenters William Edward and George Evans.

My great grandparents Thomas and Elizabeth Willis bought the Mill, and started milling in 1880. My grandparents Thomas John and Elizabeth continued after them, and my father Stanley continued into the 1950s, when milling ceased to be a profitable concern. My father was the last of the Gower millers.

Llanrhidian Lower (or Nether) Mill was the largest in the area with an 18 ft wheel, and supported two pairs of stones – one for rough grain, and one for fine flour. The French stones were the best. Dad was also a skilled millstone dresser. The stones had to be cut properly to allow the milled flour to flow smoothly.

The external structure of the building is sound, but unfortunately the inside is dilapidated and unsafe. The wheel and machinery were removed almost 50 years ago. I can just remember seeing sparks from the cutting torches as they cut up the metal wheel.

During the last war the Mill sometimes ran 24 hours a day to keep up with the constant need for flour. Thomas John and Stanley (who was in the Home Guard) would take it in turns to do the night shift. By then, my grandmother Elizabeth was doing a lot of the milling, as Thomas John was suffering from 'Miller's Lung'.

The Mill dairying industry developed as a result of the decline of the milling, and Dad's title changed from 'Stan the Mill' to 'Stan the Milk'. We raised our own heifers and produced and delivered milk to Llanrhidian and neighbouring villages until the 1970s.

Sadly, there are no millers there now, but it still remains in the same family and hopefully, will do so for a long time to come.

J. Parry Williams and Sons, Baytree House
by Marjorie Williams and Thelma Pritchard

J. Parry Williams lived in Baytree House, with his sons Parry, Kenny and Edgar. He was known as Johnnie Parry, and his eldest son as Parry Williams. They had a large garage opposite Baytree House, where Threeways is today. It had a joiner's workshop behind it where they made a wide range of items – including doors, windows and coffins. It was a busy place, and employed some local men to work there. Everyone called this area 'Parry's Cross', and still do today.

In the 1890s, Johnnie Parry worked for Bennett Bros. as a foreman when they built the new Swansea Market, with its glass and wrought iron roof. Alongside Baytree was a stable, and the horses there were used for haulage, often taking loads from Bob Jeffrey's quarry.

In Llanrhidian, Parry Williams had a mortar mill near the Quoits Field. This mortar was used in many of the walls in the village. It is black, as ash was mixed with the lime. With the approach of the Second World War, building in Gower declined, so Parry Williams went to work for Weaver's in Swansea. Whilst with this company, he helped build the aerodrome in Kidwelly, and watched the first plane land there – after some stunt flying to inaugurate it! He built Woodlands for his family, replacing the derelict house called 'Bathers' that was there, and later built Sunnytops in School Lane.

Kenny Williams, in a conversation recorded in the 1980s by Eric Morgan, recalled: "Cyril Jeffreys's father would come into Gower to buy ricks of hay. Tom Tucker's father, Uncle Tom, would cut the hay into bales with a hay knife, then we would take them into Swansea in a horse and gambo. It would take us four hours to get to Swansea. I would have a gambo, Tom Tucker would have one, and my cousin had a four-wheeler with two horses. We would take the hay to the land on which the Carlton cinema was later built, where there were stables." Kenny would also take his mother to market in a pony and trap, but describes the return journey as 'murder!' as the butchers returning to their homes in Gower after a long day in market would come galloping past. Kenny also recalled the days

Parry Williams.

The mortar mill, bottom left hand corner.

Kenny, Edgar & Haydn Parry.

when the corn would be cut with scythes, the men stopping for a lunch of bread and cheese. He quotes the saying, "Bread and cheese, work with ease!" At fourteen, Kenny went to work in Swansea, for 7/6 a week, and lodgings. He worked in an accountant's office for a year, but then decided to learn a trade, and became a carpenter. Kenny would ride home from Swansea on his pushbike.

Like his grandfather before him (Kenny's grandfather's record book showed that he had carried out 400 burials), Kenny became an undertaker, and would make coffins in the workshop adjoining the house. Thelma Pritchard recalls helping her parents to prepare the coffins. Kenny would do the carpentry work, and Patty his wife would line them with silk and lace. The coffin was then wax polished, and on the day of the funeral, Kenny would lead the procession wearing a top hat and tails.

Glyn A. Grove
(Grand Master of the Oddfellows)
Remembered by Roy Collins

My grandfather Glyn Grove was born at Newparks, Llanrhidian, in 1891 to James and Mary Grove, née Austin, the youngest of six children.

The family moved to what is now Cross House, at about the turn of the century, where Glyn's eldest sister ran the Post Office from 1934.

At 15, Glyn was a pupil teacher at Llanrhidian School, but was unable to pursue a career in teaching because he had to work in the colliery to earn a living.

At an early age he was appointed secretary of the Oddfellows 'Rock of Friendship' lodge, a position that he held until his death in 1968. At the same time he administered the National Insurance Scheme for the area. This was the forerunner of the National Health Service and was introduced by the Lloyd George Government in 1910. People would either visit Glyn at his home, or would go to the Oddfellows meetings to pay their subscriptions, but their National Insurance subscriptions were collected at his home and a card would be marked. The Oddfellows meetings were originally held at the Dolphin Inn, but later moved to the Welcome to Town.

I have many recollections of people visiting Glyn at Llwynderw to pay their 'club'. Many would come from Wernffrwd or Llanmorlais, travelling down on one bus and returning on the next, which was an hour later. To ensure that they had full value for their bus fare, some of the people would use the time they had to wait for the bus to ask Glyn to address some problem or other that they might have. But Glyn always found time to talk to them, and would sometimes end up resolving personal or financial problems for them. Obviously nobody else was privy to such discussions but we would hear much later from these people how much they had been helped.

His main work as a young man was felling trees at Penrice Estate for the mines, and as a collier. These were both reserved occupations during World War I. At the time of his marriage to Mary Austin in 1917, he was working as a collier at Gilfach Goch colliery, coming home at weekends to stay with his wife's family at Newton Farm. He also worked at the Lynch colliery for a year and the Western colliery. In 1922, Glyn and his family moved to Llwynderw and he took up farming part-time until he finished working in the colliery in 1925/6, to make farming his full-time occupation.

His four children, Glenis (Lucas), Wilma (Collins), Will and Olga (Evans), were all brought up in Llwynderw, and the family is living there now. In 1929, Glyn was elected Councillor for Llanrhidian Lower Parish Council, and appointed clerk to the Council in 1937. His father, James was also elected to these positions in 1894.

Glyn was elected to the Gower Rural District Council in 1934, and appointed Justice of the Peace in 1949. He served as a Magistrate at Penmaen and Gowerton for many years. He was also on the Board of Governors for what was then the Glamorgan Education Authority, and attended regular meetings in County Hall, Cardiff.

Glyn eventually served as Chairman of the Gower Rural District Council and as Grand Master of the Oddfellows.

The Brickyard
Remembered by Ernie Grove

The brickyard was in the field just past the cattle grid on the Marsh road. It belonged to Will 'Nancy', and the bricks are in the chimneys round about here today. The field had clay in it, and they would also bake the bricks down there.

The 1920 Schedule of the land for sale by the Penrice Estate includes the brickfield. It records that it is let to William Williams, known to everyone in Llanrhidian as 'Will Nancy'.

LOT 76.

(Coloured *Pink* on Plan No. 4).

ALL THAT FREEHOLD ENCLOSURE OF PASTURE LAND

known as

BRICKFIELD

situate on Llanrhidian Marsh, Nod. 408 and 409 on Ordnance Map 1915 Edition, for the Parish of Llanrhidian Lower, containing an area of

3a. 1r. 17p.

or thereabouts. Let for six months to 29th September 1920 to William Williams at a rent of £1 15s. 0d. for the period.

The Tithe Rent Charge apportionment on this Lot amounts to 6s. 6d., and is payable by the Owner.

Schedule for the sale of the brickyard.

Betsy Williams, Herbalist
Remembered by Nancy Payne, née Dunn

In the 1900s, my great grandfather, Johnnie Williams, lived in Old Mill Cottage, Llanrhidian. His first wife was Nancy and they had three children, one of whom was William. William Williams was a very common name, so everyone in Llanrhidian knew him as Will Nancy. When Nancy died, Johnnie married again – this time to my great granny Betsy.

Granny Betsy was a herbalist and grew a great variety of plants and herbs in the garden at Old Mill Cottage – nettles, dandelions and stone parsley grew in abundance, as did elder trees as she would use both the

*Five generations of the Williams family, Old Mill Cottage.
From left: Johnnie Williams, his daughter Elizabeth Ann, his father George Williams holding baby Stanley Willis, and Elizabeth his granddaughter.*

bark and flowers for her potions and medicines. People would come to the cottage where she would give them her various tonics.

Betsy was present at the beginning and ending of many lives in Llanrhidian, acting as midwife to many of the mothers in the village, and she was always sent for when there had been a death in a family.

THE LIMEKILN
Remembered by Kenny Williams

There was a limekiln outside the church hall on the hill. A Jubilee rail ran from the quarries to the kiln. There was a lot of lime produced for the farmers' fields. I remember that Ivor Parry fell into the kiln, and they had to get him out before the fumes got to him.

Billy Thomas owned one quarry, and Tom Tucker had another. There was a man named Morris, who lived in a cottage near the top quarry. He had a tool for scraping the mud off the road. We called it 'Morris's piano'.

We would go to Hill's Farm, Llanmadoc, in a horse and trap to fetch a hundred weight of sand, as many houses and the pubs in Llanrhidian put sand on their floors. The village boys would sift through the discarded sand outside the pubs, looking for any silver thruppenny bits that might have been dropped.

QUARRYING AND ROAD BUILDING
Recalled by Ernie Grove

Quarrying was carried out in the village when I was a boy. We called it 'Bob's Quarry', as it belonged to Bob Jeffreys. When they were blasting in the quarry, they would hold us back when we were coming home from school. I remember trucks there and a crusher to crush stones for road building. The lorries would dump a load of stone where it was needed. Then there were the roadmen – my father Oliver Grove was one – each man working a length. It was their job to maintain the gutters, fill in the potholes and keep the water off the road.

I remember when the village was tarred for the first time. I was going down to Parry's Cross where we had a cow stall, with my sister Elsie. A roller from Ilston had brought a load of stones and clay to level the road ready for the tarmac, but there was a flood and we couldn't cross the road. The stones were washed down to Parry's Cross – and as far as the Mill. Uncle Austin was a couple of days hauling it from there with a horse and cart. That was a flood, I can tell you!

They would use a scraper to fill in the potholes before the tarmac was put on, and a knapping hammer to break the stone down. The foundations of the road were blocked stone, pitched at an angle, one behind the other, and then the roller would squeeze them tight. My Uncle Austin used to do the Marsh road, which often floods in high tide. Frank Shepherd told me that he remembered when the tide reached the gate of our house (Millbrook Cottage), but the highest tide I remember was when the water reached the gate to the pumping station, and Stanley Willis had to go down to rescue his pigs that he kept in a shed in the field there. That was the tide that came over the road in Penclawdd that morning, and our gang were called out to put up barriers. Since then they have built a wall. I remember seeing a mouse that had climbed onto a piece of wood floating in the schoolyard there!

When the road by the school was tarmaced, the tarmac came from Ilston quarry. That was good tarmac! It was brought by Sentinels – steam driven lorries that brought ten-ton loads. Imagine a steam engine bringing a load like that up Llethrid hill. Very powerful!

Four generations of the Williams family, 'Johnnie the Jockey', Sidney, Terry and Peter.

SIDNEY WILLIAMS, BUILDER
by Terry Williams

My grandfather John Williams was known as 'Johnnie The Jockey'. He kept a smallholding in Nantywrach, which he had built himself, gathering the sand from Wernffrwd. He also had a stallion, which he would take around West Wales, for stud. My grandfather would ride a pony, whilst leading the stallion.

My father, Sidney Williams, of Rocklea, built many of the houses in Llanrhidian, including his own home, and the houses and flats in Malt Hall. He also worked on the halls and churches in Llangennith and Reynoldston, and built the church hall in Llanrhidian.

When Thomas John Willis, the miller, died, he had left a letter telling his family that Sidney Williams was to make his coffin. From then onwards, my father became an undertaker as well as a builder. He would do all types of carpentry work in his workshop, but his friend who lived nearby was always able to tell if he was making a coffin, from the sound that the saw made on the wood. He would soon be down to ask, "Who's died?"

The Opening of the Church Hall, 21st November 1934.
From left: Emlyn Perkins, Mrs. Olwen Jones, Sidney J. Williams, builder, Miss Flora Jeffreys, Mrs. H. Gordon, E. Harris, Rev. Ben Jones, Miss B. Jeffreys, Mrs. Mary Jeffreys, Cyril Grove, carpenter, Arthur Williams, carpenter, Mrs. E. Williams, Mr. Kent, policeman, Mrs. Beynon Penrhallt, and a labourer.

NEW CHURCH HALL, LLANRHIDIAN.

The Opening Ceremony

OF THE ABOVE WILL TAKE PLACE ON

WEDNESDAY, NOV. 21st, 1934, at 5 p.m.

WHEN THE

Right Rev. The Lord Bishop of the Diocese,
The Ven. Archdeacon of Gower,

AND OTHERS WILL TAKE PART.

The Vicar and Churchwardens cordially invite you to be present.

TEA PROVIDED.

An invitation to the Opening Ceremony.

The sheep wash, Cefn Bryn.

Sheep

by Ernie Grove

My father, Oliver Grove, kept sheep on the marsh and on the Bryn. The Bryn sheep were 'as wild as hawks' but the marsh sheep were gentle, nudging you if they wanted to be fed. Many people owned sheep on the marsh, but it was easy to separate your flock from the others. If you walked along quietly, they would follow you – they knew who was in their flock! Foot rot was a problem in those days, so I would bring the flock to the Horseshoe Pond where they were enclosed, and I would trim their hooves. My father would make his way to the marsh, chewing a wad of tobacco. He would then spit into the trimmed hoof, and it would act as a disinfectant. I was allowed out of school early when it was high tide, to bring the sheep off the marsh. We would only bring them in on a very high tide – they knew if they stayed on the bank the sea wouldn't reach them.

The flock that we kept on the Bryn would always have gritty wool, from Talbot's Way we thought. Every year we would wash them. Other farmers would be there with their flocks too. We would pen the sheep in to start, using hurdles we had taken with us, then there would be two lines of rope leading to the sheep wash. We would have stopped up any holes there, and the water would be quite deep. My father would put on an old suit and get into the water – it would be about chest high – and my job was to catch the sheep using a rope with a loop on it. I would put the rope around their necks and let them swim through the wash. After the sheep were washed, the wool would rise and be easier for shearing. We would bring the sheep down to the stall for shearing. My father would hand shear them – he was very good at it! Then we would mark them with our sign – ours was OG for Oliver Grove. We'd have a fire going, with a cast iron pot of tar, and would dip the sign into the tar and dab it on their sides. All the sheep also had to have an ear mark. Ours was a half ha'penny on one ear, and a slit on the other. Dipping was compulsory in those days, and Mr. Moon, the policeman, would always be there to time how long the sheep were under the water.

Frank Harry, Cobbler
Remembered by Roy Grey

Frank Harry was a cobbler, and I remember that he would drink tea out of a basin. He lived in Berwick Cottage with his sisters, Mary and Margaret. He would come down to Big House whenever we killed a pig.

He would pour boiling water over the pig to scrape the hairs off after it had been killed. He would then collect them all together, and use them for sewing the shoes, I should think.

He was a bit cantankerous! I remember when there were carol singers outside his house. He opened his bedroom window, and in his night-shirt shouted down, "How many are you, boys?"

"Four, Mr. Harry," the boys replied hopefully. He then poured the contents of his chamber pot over them saying, "There! Share that between you!"

Game Keeping
by Dick Beynon

When I left school at 14, I went to work in Wernhalog Woods. The woods around here were all owned by Admiral Heneage, and leased out. Mr. Gees was the head gamekeeper there. I would work seven days a week for 10 shillings and a suit of clothes. I was also given a gun and cartridges.

The gamekeepers in those days kept hawks to keep off predators, but there were no foxes around then, so the wild pheasants had a good chance of survival, but pheasants are bad mothers, as long as there is one chick following them, they will leave the others.

My first job was to go around with a horse and trap buying cluck hens. These are hens that are getting ready to sit. We would take them back to the pens, and give them a good delousing with powder, as a hen will not sit if its lousy. Each hen would sit on about a dozen pheasants' eggs. These would be brought from England and would be delivered in hampers, with the eggs carefully packed. A year before, we would have prepared the ground where the pens were going to be, checking for stoats and weasels. When the chicks had hatched, we stayed there for six weeks – day and night – to care for them. They would be fed on hard-boiled eggs and rice. We would also get money from the skins of any stoats, weasels and moles that we caught. We usually netted them so that we would not damage the skin. It was a messy job to skin them, but then a good moleskin with no blemish could be sold for 3d-4d.

We would also catch rabbits, and on a Friday evening I could go around the village with twelve rabbits and have no problem selling them. A good rabbit would fetch 4d. There were a lot of hungry people around then, and it might be the only food that some people could afford. The other animal skins would be sent away. All the money went in a pot – a large glass bowl, and at Christmas time it would be shared out. I would receive about £25. A lot of money in those days.

There was some poaching, of course. Mr. Gees went to one farm, where there was a lovely smell of cooking. He stayed there quite a while, and when he left, the bird that had been roasting had been completely burned. They couldn't take it out when he was there, as he would have known it was one of his birds! If you were a tenant of the Penrice Estate, in a tied cottage and you were caught poaching, you would lose your job and home. One farmer got around this by feeding the birds Indian corn laced with whisky. This made the birds dopey and easy to catch. He was never caught out!

When it was time for the shoot, we would go around hiring beaters. Everyone wanted to be a beater as they would be paid 5 shillings a day – some were only getting that for a week's work. About 200 birds would be killed in a day's shoot. Admiral Heneage kept Cillibion Wood for the woodcock. We would shoot those woods after a week or so of hard frost. Dogs often didn't like to retrieve woodcock, but if the beaters found a dead woodcock, they would take the two pin feathers and leave the bird to be picked up later. You could sell a pair of pin feathers for 5 shillings. They would be used in artist's brushes. The woodcock were considered difficult birds to shoot, and the number of pin feathers that they had were considered a source of pride to the sportsmen.

It was calculated that each pheasant in those days cost £1 to produce. During the shoot, the gentry would enjoy lunch prepared for them in a local farmhouse, whilst the beaters ate in a nearby shed. The privately owned farms here would rent out their fields to the estate, so that the men could shoot any pheasants that travelled over them. Mr. Gees would see that they got a bottle of whisky and three brace of pheasants a year. But it all changed after his day.

Later on, I had a dog that I trained to 'pick up' the fallen birds. It was my job to stand behind the guns and then send the dog to retrieve the pheasants. I would be paid 10 shillings a day for this. We would also train ferrets to catch rabbits. On a wet day, we would spend a long time handling the young ferrets and getting them used to being touched and would then send them down the rabbit holes.

BEATING

by Ernie Grove

First of all, they would hire us to go beating. Us boys, this side of Penmaen would 'stop' as they say, in the swede fields – stop the pheasants running out of the woods. We would be planted in different places, and the men from over the other side – Penmaen – would be beating towards us, and the shotsmen would be in between. I remember 250 birds shot in

Beating in Parc le Breos woods.
Dick Beynon in centre of photo, with a long stick.

Parc le Breos laid out in the yard. They had a wagon and horse, picking the birds up. In my opinion, it was cruel. The birds were well fed – the keepers would feed them and see that the foxes didn't get them, but they wouldn't climb as sharp as a wild pheasant.

We started at Llethrid and Cillibion and the boys from Penmaen would almost catch us up, with the shotsmen in between, and afterwards we would be directed to different places to shoot out a wood. We used to beat up around Malt House, near Llethrid. They would be shooting for woodcock there because the river went up that way and the land was damp.

The Toffs were the shotsmen – well-to-do men. We used to get 5 shillings a day beating – good money for us. Five bob was what we had for a week's work! Sometimes they would give us a bottle of beer and bread and cheese. There were so many pheasants that the shotsmen would be firing all the time. The estate, owned a lot of land around here – they owned this hill here in Llanrhidian.

Nancy Payne, née Dunn, remembers . . .
Shoots were often held around my home when I lived at Pengwern Farm with my parents, and Admiral Heneage would come to make arrangements with them. He would take over our front room for the week of the shoot, and my parents had to provide a warm fire, and white cloths for the tables.

Admiral Heneage's butler would arrive with baskets of food, and during the shoot the Admiral and the gentry would enjoy a fine meal. The beaters stayed outside. Later my parents would be thanked with a brace of pheasants.

Market Gardening

By the 1920s, Swansea Market had 670 stalls, many selling meat, fruit and vegetables from Gower. Many families in Llanrhidian grew produce for the market. Every Saturday, Richie Shepherd and his wife Margaret would go to market to sell meat, vegetables and watercress from their beds in Stavel Hagar, and Dora Jones would go three times a week, taking produce that her husband Leonard had grown in their garden. By the time that Dora returned home from market, Leonard would have replanted the beds that had been emptied that morning.

Wilma Collins took produce to market, as did her grandmother Annie Austin had done before her. Annie would go in with her son Ambrose who was a butcher. The butchers' stalls were against the wall in the market, and had their own fireplaces where Annie would cook sausages or chops for their dinner.

Ernie Grove remembers the Sumley apple that was only grown in Llanrhidian. The villagers would take baskets of apples to market in the Vanguard bus. The single decker bus would stop at The Cross, and the driver, Joe Hoskins, would climb up the ladder at the back, and lower down a rope for the baskets to be attached, and then would draw them up with a hook. There was a rail around the top of the bus to secure the baskets.

In the market, the traders who did not have stalls would sit on boxes, surrounded by their wares. They were known as 'the squatters'. Wilma remembers the poverty of the times – a man who had lost both his arms in the First World War stood at the market entrance selling matches, a tray hanging from a cord around his neck, and the little boys without shoes asking for orange boxes which they would chop up and sell for firewood.

The market closed at 9 p.m. There were always two bells that rang to warn customers that the market was closing. Some people waited until after the first bell to do their shopping, hoping to get cheaper produce then. Incendiary bombs extensively damaged the market in February 1941, and the traders had to move out. They eventually returned after being in temporary accommodation, and in 1961 the new market was opened, and still provides produce from Gower.

The Wheelwright's Shop and Forge
by Audrey Williams

When I was a child, I spent many happy hours in the wheelwright's shop, which was situated in Oldwalls, on the land that now belongs to Lyndon Tucker.

My father and grandfather worked there repairing carts, wains and wheelbarrows, and even making new ones. My uncle Will who was the blacksmith worked in the smithy next door. Therefore this was an ideal place for the farmers and smallholders to meet and have their vehicles repaired.

Can you imagine what news and bits of information were exchanged there, for although some farmers came from neighbouring villages, others would have travelled quite a distance?

I found it very fascinating to watch my father make a wheel. When it

National Master Farriers' Association.

Registered Office:—10, Upper Fountaine Street, Leeds.

SWANSEA BRANCH.

President:
W. JONES ANSTEY, A.F.C.L.
Secretary:
D. CARSON, A.F.C.L.

Telegrams:
"FARRIERS," LEEDS.

DEAR SIR,
In consequence of the considerable increase in Materials—Coal, Iron, Nails, Breezes, also the important advance in Men's Wages, the above Branch has been compelled to revise their Price List as below from July 1st, 1915. Customers are requested to take notice of the revised Price List and Rules of Forges, in order to avoid disputes when accounts are rendered.

Minimum Price List for Horse Shoeing.

Description	Per set of Plain Shoes	Square Stud Holes Per Hole	Screwed Stud Holes ½–1 Each	Bar Shoes Extra per set	Roughing New Shoes Extra pr set	Removing Ordinary	Removing and Roughing	Frost Nails	Leather and Stopping Extra per pr	Stopp'g with Old Leather Per Pair	Frog Pads & Stopping Per Pair	Old Shoes Each
Donkeys and Mules	3 6	...	...	0 6	0 6	2 0	2 3	1 3	...	...	...	0 6
Ponies	4 0	1½	2d.	0 6	0 9	2 6	2 6	1 6	2 0	1 0	3 0	0 9
Trade, Cab and Cobs	4 6	1½	2d.	0 6	1 0	2 6	3 0	1 6	2 6	1 0	3 6	0 9
Light Cart and Van	5 0	1½	2d.	1 0	1 0	3 0	3 0	1 6	2 6	1 0	3 6	1 0
Heavy Cart and Dray	5 6	1½	2d.	1 0	1 0	3 6	3 3	1 9	2 9	1 4	4 6	1 0
Heavy Draught	6 0	1½	2d.	1 3	1 0	3 6	3 6	1 9	2 9	1 4	4 6	1 0
Carriage and Hackneys	6 0	1½	2d.	1 3	1 0	3 6	3 6	1 9	2 9	1 4	4 6	1 0
Light Entires	...	...	...	...	...	5 0	...	...	...	...	...	...
Cart Horse Entires	10 0	...	...	...	...	5 0	...	...	...	...	...	...
Heavy Draught Entires	15 0	...	...	...	...	6 0	...	...	...	...	...	...

Show Horses 2/6 per set extra. All Colts, 2/- per set extra. Toe Pieces—Iron 3d., Steel 4d. each.

Vicious Horses extra according to number of men and time over 1½ hours and if in Stocks.

Studs must be purchased from Farrier to fit holes. Accounts, Monthly Strictly Nett (Contracts extra.)

Shoes not bearing registered Trade Mark (Anvil Stamp) will be charged extra.

Business Hours from   a.m. to   p.m., Saturdays a.m. to   p.m. All overtime is discouraged and will be charged extra.

While every care and precaution will be taken the owner of the establishment accepts no responsibility with regard to accident to horses while being-shod or taken home which is gratuitous and is not part of his contract.

RULES OF FORGES

1. Customers are requested to refrain from talking to workmen during working hours upon any subject likely to cause any hindrance.

2. All Complaints are to be made to the Masters (or man in charge during his absence.)

3. No work executed on Sundays and Public Holidays except to relieve pain, and which is charged extra.

4. All acholic drinks are strictly forbidden in forge and customers are requested not to ask workmen to leave the forge for drinks during working hours. Any workman under influence of drink will be dismissed.

CORRUPTION ACT, 1906.—The owner of the establishment refrains from Christmas Boxes, or any other form of gratuities.

Smoking strictly prohibited during working hours.

Thanking you for past favours and soliciting a continuance of same,

THE SECRETARY.

Bert Dunn was given this price list for farriers, July 1915, when he began his apprenticeship at Oldwalls forge.

Outside the wheelwright's shop and forge, Oldwalls.

was completed, it would be taken next door, where my uncle would place the hot iron bands around it, then plunge it into the pool which was outside the blacksmith's door – the iron bands would then contract and tighten around the wheel.

Later, my uncle started another business. He bought a shed opposite the forge, and sold a variety of interesting articles there, including coconut mats, tin cans, paraffin, linseed oil, nails and screws. I think this venture was started when tractors were introduced into Gower, and there was not such a demand for horses to do the farm work. He still shod the occasional horse, and made horseshoes.

One thing I remember vividly, you could take your wireless batteries there to be charged. Most people would have several of these batteries, one to use whilst the other one was on charge in my uncle's shop. One had to be very careful carrying these batteries, because if they leaked the acid would burn a hole in your clothes.

The Sawmills, Cillibion

Phillip Jones established the sawmills at Black Lane, Cillibion, in 1917. On the other side of Black Lane was the blacksmith's forge. The smith on the 1901 census was Samuel Williams, aged 47.

The sawmills, Cillibion.

Phillip built the sawmills to provide work for his five sons – George, Ted, Stan, John and Harold.

The sawmill produced gambos and carts, and as the making of wheels was a specialised craft, Phillip also employed wheelwrights. The mill traded under the name 'Jones Bros.' and at first were sawyers – felling trees, and using an A frame to lift and manoeuvre the logs into position on the rack bench ready for sawing. The timber would be stored until it was needed for gates, gambos and fences. A band saw was used for the finer work like cutting patterns for wheelbarrows and the spokes and fellies for wheels. The traction engine in the background was used to power the saw.

Later they owned a thrasher and trusser, and travelled to farms on the outskirts of Swansea, to thrash the corn and truss the sheaves. The sawdust would be sold for use in butchers' shops and to cover the floors of cattle trucks. In 1926, Phillip died, and the sawmills continued trading under the name of Stanley Jones.

Four of the sons of Phillip Jones – George, Ted, Stan and John.

A gambo and cart.
(Photograph by kind permission of Tom and Elizabeth Roderick).

THE SAWMILLS
Remembered by Roger Jones

When I was living in Cillibion, the sawmills made farm implements. Stanley Jones never minded me hanging around watching gambos being made and the fascinating job of putting an iron tyre on a wooden wheel. When the sawmills were not too busy, Stanley and Tom Pearce made wheelbarrows – in those days entirely of ash and oak, with a wooden wheel and iron tyre.

Christie Tucker, Chauffeur
by Rosemary Beynon

My father Christie Tucker of Brynview, Llanrhidian, became a chauffeur to the Morris family, Cae Forgan. Mr. Morris was the county coroner. Mrs. Morris asked my father to take their car to Oldwalls on a trial run, and when he returned, she said, "Now you can take me to Swansea!" He stayed with the family for some years, driving and taking care of their cars.

Christie Tucker at Cae Forgan.

The Morris family, Cae Forgan.

His experience in Cae Forgan came in useful in his next job – he went to work for Llewellyn Gordon, driving his traction engine. He and Sam Winch would drive all over Gower using the engine for thrashing.*

Thrashing was a winter activity, and it was an impressive sight to see the thrasher drawn by a steam engine being taken around Gower. The team would spend a day thrashing and then move on to the next farm. Sam Winch and Christie Tucker were the drivers for Llewellyn Gordon. The farmers would provide wood, coal and water, and it would take a while to get 'steam up'. The driver would then blow his whistle to let the neighbouring farmers know that their help was needed. Thrashing was a communal activity, needing a lot of hands to complete the work.

The thrasher was parked near the corn ricks, and men were needed to pitch the sheaves onto the machine. Two men would be standing on the top of the thrasher in sunken bays. One would take the sheaves from the men working on the rick. He would cut the binding, and pass them to the second man who fed them headfirst into the thrasher. The grain and chaff were separated, and the straw was ejected. The straw was laid down to form a new rick, so as one rick was depleted of corn, another rick of straw was being built. This would be used for animal bedding. Other men were needed to carry away the bags of grain to the lofts for

---

* Always spelt and pronounced thrashing in Llanrhidian.

Mary Gordon and friend in front of Llewellyn Gordon's traction engine and thrasher.
(Photograph provided by Sylvia Hughes).

*Llewellyn Gordon, Highbury, Dick Jeffreys, Llwyn y bwch,
and Thomas Clement, Freedown.*

storage. This was the most strenuous task. Behind the thrasher was a trusser, which was used to truss the straw into bundles ready to be used to thatch the ricks.

It was a busy time for the women of the farm, as it was a matter of pride to serve the thrashing team with ample quantities of the best quality food.

Ernie Grove recalls that farmers, who lived in farms at the end of long muddy tracks, would take the opportunity of a visit from the traction engine to get a pile of stones. These they would lay across the track, so that they would be crushed by the steam engine, and a new road would be easily laid.

Glyn Rogers, Kennexstone Farm, remembers that it was a busy day at the farm when Christie Tucker arrived with the engine and thrasher. There would be about fifteen men helping with the thrashing, and after work they would all sit down to a hearty meal. The men would discuss the meals that had been prepared for them in the farms they had visited. He recalled one man saying, "In the last farm, we had rabbits in ankle socks!" They hadn't been completely skinned before cooking.

Thrashing day was a busy day for Glyn's terrier Bonzo too. He knew when the corn was moved there would be plenty of rats around. He was an expert at catching and killing them. The next day, the engine would have moved to another farm, but when the whistle blew, Bonzo would disappear over the fields in the direction of the whistle – ready for another day's hunting!

Mary Gordon and friend in front of a corn rick at Highbury.
(Photograph provided by Sylvia Hughes).

In the 1940s, the invention of the combine harvester produced a machine that could cut wheat, thrash it and collect the grain in its tanks. One man driving a combine harvester could do the work of many.

The first powered combine harvester in Gower, Llanrhidian, 1949. Master – Llewellyn Gordon, driver – Freddie Bowen, Burry Green and bagger Ronnie Tucker, Llanrhidian.

1932. The John family, Tyrcoed, enjoy a break in the harvest field. In front of Bess the horse are (from left to right) George Grove, 18, Elwyn B. John, 12, Mrs. Gladys M. John, Gethin D. John, 18 months, Mr. Oswald P. John, and Richie Williams, 21.

Ivor Parry and friends.

Leighton Pritchard with a horse drawn hay rake.

PLOUGHING IN LLANRHIDIAN

Ploughing matches have been part of the rural scene in Gower for many years, and the *Cambrian* newspaper carries many detailed descriptions of the proceedings.

November 2nd, 1849
The ploughing match for the Western District took place on Thursday, the 25th at Parkyrrhedyn in the parish of Llanrhidian. Eighteen teams started, sixteen men and two boys. The ploughing gave much satisfaction and was very creditably performed. The first prize was awarded to Thomas Austin, ploughman to

> **Llanrhidian Ploughing Match Society.**
>
> THE SECOND ANNUAL PLOUGHING MATCH will take place on the Farm of Mr. GEORGE TUCKER, Partyrhedin, in the Parish of Llanrhidian Lower,
>
> ON TUESDAY, MARCH 5th 1867,
>
> when the following Prizes will be awarded, viz :—
>
> Class I.—Open to all comers. 1st Prize, £2 10s.; 2nd, £1.
>
> Class II.—Open to Subscribers within the Parish only. 1st Prize, £2; 2nd, £1 10s.; 3rd, £1; 4th, 10s.
>
> Class III — Open to Subscribers within the Parish only, for Boys under 18 years of age. 1st Prize, 15s.; 2nd, 10s.; 3rd, 5s.
>
> All Entries to be made in writing to the Secretary, on or before Saturday, March 2nd. Entrance fee, 5s.
>
> All competitors to be on the ground not later than 9 o'clock.
>
> RICHARD DUNN, Secretary, Leason, Gower.
>
> A DINNER will be provided in the Evening, at the WELCOME TO TOWN, Llanrhidian. Tickets, 2s. each.

Ploughing match, 1867.

J. H. Vivian Esq., the second to David Long, ploughman to Mr. W. Davies, Penrhallt, and the third to William Tall, ploughman to C. Morgan, Caeforgan.

On the 25th March 1870, a match was organised by the secretary of the West Gower Society, Richard Dunn of Leason. In this article the writer records: '. . . *when the business was over at the field, the judges, stewards and friends to the success of the plough repaired to the Dolphin Inn, Llanrhidian, where a substantial dinner had been prepared. After numerous toasts, the awards were handed out. 1st prize for all-comers – William Tall. 1st prize for district – Mr. Gordon, Llwynybwch.*'

On the 9th February 1872, there was a match at two fields in Llanrhidian. One at Llethrid and the other at Killibion.

At nine o'clock in the morning, five and twenty teams entered the fields fully caparisoned, and presenting a grand appearance. After the match, a dinner was provided at the Dolphin Inn. Mr. Bowen, Llythrid, supplied refreshments, and his amiable daughter Kate regaled the hardy sons of toil with Cwrw Da. 1st prize – William Tall, Llanrhidian, £2. 10s. 2nd prize – George Jenkins, Calivor, £1.

It was a wealthy farmer who could afford a 'double tom' but the expense would have saved a lot of work. The double tom was a ridging plough that would have cut both ways, whilst a farmer with an ordinary plough would have had twice the work to do.

A 'double tom' plough.
(Photograph by kind permission of Stuart Clayfield).

In 1991, A. Ellis Davies, Llanrhidian, wrote *The Golden Furrow*, a history of the West Gower Ploughing Society, and in it he describes the different types of ploughing:

High Cut Ploughing
High Cut ploughing consists of narrow, tightly packed unbroken furrows, which have a high combe, and are almost equal in width and length and resemble equilateral triangles. This type of ploughing was used initially for sowing corn by hand, before mechanisation. The seed fell into the bottom of the triangle, and then was brushed over with the harrow, thus causing the high crest of the

North Gower 1940, Ivor Parry, Llanrhidian, watches as his son Willie competes in a ploughing match.

furrow to break down, and seal the grain, which would later grow up in the drills left by the plough.

Digger or Chilled Ploughing
Digger or chilled ploughing is a wider, more broken furrow, which buries the weed and stubble more easily, and needs less cultivating to make a seedbed. This type of ploughing is ideal for spring ploughing.

General Purpose Ploughing
This is a type of ploughing which is adaptable to lea or stubble, and is a half way style between high cut and digger ploughing. It was very popular during the war years, and also in the post war years until 1960, and is suitable for autumn ploughing.

Ellis Davies winning the Boys Class at one of his first ploughing matches at Little Reynoldston Farm, in 1956.

From these early beginnings, Ellis went on to compete in many ploughing competitions, and in 1967 he became Champion Ploughman of Wales. He repeated his success in 1968, and again in 1981. In 1982 came the pinnacle of his ploughing career when he became High Cut Ploughing Champion of Great Britain. Ellis is on the World Board of Ploughing, and is a Director of the Welsh Ploughing Association.

Corn mows at Lunnon, Gower.
(Photograph by kind permission of the Jones family, Lunnon).

RICK BUILDING AND THATCHING IN GOWER
by A. Ellis Davies

In the days before mechanisation, corn was cut by hand with the scythe, and tied into sheaves. It was the men's job to cut the corn and the women did the binding. Between 1880-1900, the reaper and binder that cut the corn and bound the sheaves came into use. The stooks were left in the fields after cutting for 'three church bells' giving them time to ripen. The stooks would then be pulled over with the butts facing the sun to dry, and then were gathered up on a horse and gambo and taken to the rickyard. Rushes or trashings of hedges and brambles were laid down to keep the corn off the floor. Then rick building could begin. This was the job for an experienced farmer, as the correct position in which the sheaves were laid was a specialised skill.

The rick builder would begin in the centre with the sheaves being laid flat – the sheaf head facing to the centre, and the butt end facing outwards. He would gradually work his way outward by lapping one sheaf on the next at approximately a 30% angle. This was important when you got to the outside, so that any rain would be drained off and not run into the rick and soak the grain. After the rick builder had finished once around the outside, he would restart in the centre and go over the process time and time again, with the rick slowly gaining height. Depending on the size of the rick, the square (sometimes called the ovis) would be about 9-10 feet high. At this point, the builder would have to pull in a little in order to create a 45% angle for the head of the rick, which would resemble a house top. This is where the greatest skill came in keeping the angle the same both sides to finish up with a true house top.

Several times between unloading, the rick builder would go down to floor level and walk around the rick casting his eye over it to see if it was true and not listing a little to one side or the other, and whether any adjustment had to be made. When it came to the turn of a younger man to start making rick – (if round they were normally called 'mows') – the experienced hand would generally stay at ground level giving advice, as the job progressed. "Squeeze out on these yer corner, boy!" or " Pull in a bit yer boy," and so on.

Sometimes, if too much beer or cider had been drunk, the mow may list to one side rather heavily, and if that happened a strut or two would have to be put into the mow to stop it toppling over. When this occurred, it was frowned upon and led to leg pulling from the neighbours.

When the head of the rick pulled in to about 3 ft. wide, a load of rush or loose straw would go on to cap the rick off. It was then raked down and left to set before thatching would commence.

Thatching
Once the harvest was complete, the ricks or mows whether hay or corn, had to be thatched. This was a task that had to be done correctly or else prolonged rain would soak through the thatch, and ruin the hay and grain underneath.

The thatch used was sometimes rush off the marsh, sometimes reed cut from Oxwich marsh. Cutting reed was a miserable job, because it had to be done by hand, often up to your knees in water, then put into bundles, tied and finally loaded up and carted home. But the most common type of thatch used in Gower was wheat straw known as 'gloy'.

This process began the previous season when the wheat was being thrashed. A machine called a trusser was attached to the rear of the thrashing machine, which tied the loose straw coming out of the machine into bundles, which were then made into the gloy rick. This was made for the following season's thatching. In the summer months before or after hay making, depending on time available, you had to draw gloy. This was done by taking down the trusses one by one from the gloy rick, cutting them open and then taking out any loose chaff and small bits of straw until you were left with only straight stiff clean straw, which was then rebundled into sheaves and tied by hand. The next job was to go to the wood and spend a day or two cutting spars. Spars were hazel sticks, cut approximately 2ft 6ins. to 3 ft. long, and about 1 inch thick, and should be as straight as possible. These were then put into bundles of 30-40 and tied. It took several hundred spars to thatch a rick.

One person could thatch unaided, but normally a younger person would tend the thatcher with gloy and spars as needed. This saved the thatcher going up and down the ladder all the while, and gave the youngster a chance to see the art being done at first hand. The thatch was put on the rick about 4 inches thick, and at about 2ft 6ins. wide at a time. At this width, the thatcher could reach quite easily off the ladder. Once the first patch at the lower end of the head was completed, the thatcher would go two or more rungs up the ladder and then repeat the process, overlapping the lower piece of thatch like laying tiles. It would take approximately 8 lengths of gloy to reach the peak. Then the spars would come into play. A spar would be pushed into the rick horizontally at each overlap in order to tie the thatching cord that held the thatch in place. Thatching cord could be bought at local ironmongers or agricultural dealers. Some farmers used binder twine, and latterly baler twine was sometimes used.

When one section was completed, the ladder would be moved over another 2ft 6ins., and then the process would continue until the thatcher had worked his way around the rick. It would take about three days to thatch a rick. Finally a sheep shears would be used to clip the top and bottom edge of the head in a straight line to make the job look neat and tidy. Although thatching was a slow, time consuming job, great pride was taken and no corners were ever cut.

Butter and Cheese Making
by Janie Hutin

I grew up on Freedown Farm, which was a mixed farm – arable, with cattle, sheep, pigs and some poultry. It was a family farm, so everybody did all the jobs. That was my grandparents, Thomas and Esther Clement, my parents Richard (Dick) and Elizabeth (Bessie) Clement, and my sister Betty and myself. As a child, I remember butter and cheese being made. We reared calves, which were later sold as store cattle in Gowerton mart. The calves were taken from their mothers' and given skimmed milk along with the usual food when old enough. The cows were milked twice a day. The milk was put into a machine called a separator – a

The Clement family, Freedown Farm.

machine that separates cream from milk. It had a round metal container on the top into which the milk was poured. Below was the mechanism; there were two tube-like pipes leading from it, one tube taking milk, and the other cream that went into separate containers. It was worked by turning a handle at the side.

    The cream was kept until the time to put it in the butter churn to make the butter, which was usually done once a week. The churn was a wooden container with a cover, which had a small window in it, to see when the butter was ready. The butter churn was turned by hand, with a handle at the side of the frame. It was a long job sometimes depending on the quality of the cream. If you wanted your butter to have a better colour, especially during the winter months, butter colour was added to the cream. Once the cream had turned to butter, it was taken out of the churn, leaving the buttermilk behind. This was usually fed to the pigs. The butter was then put into a butter worker. A handle at the side turned it, with all the buttermilk being pressed out by the roller.

Once this was completed, it was put into another wooden container to be mixed with salt, and then weighed into pounds and half pounds. Some people just squared the butter with a grooved wooden butter print. Ours was put into a wooden mould, with a butter stamp that was carved for stamping patterns on the butter. Ours was three heads of wheat. In the summer time, if the weather was hot or thundery, the cream would be put overnight to stand in very cold water from our well. The butter then would not be too soft to handle.

If we had milk to spare, my grandmother would make cheese. That milk would not be separated, it would be put into bowls for the cream to rise to the top. It was skimmed next day, and added to some fresh milk to be made into cheese. It would be put into a large earthenware vessel and the cheese rennet added. After a time, it would become solid, the curds were cut up and the whey drained off. The curds would be mixed with salt and put in a cheese vat. This was a round wooden container with holes in the bottom, lined with cheesecloth. The cheese vat would then be put on a cheese press, a tall iron implement. It had a flat round grooved bottom on which the cheese vat was placed. Above was a flat piece, which was turned down onto the cheese by a handle. This was turned a little at a time to press the curds solid and all whey drained off.

Once this process was completed, the cheese would be taken out of the vat, and left to dry, making a softish rind all around. It had to be turned often, so that it would dry evenly. I am not certain how long it was left to dry, as we would be anxious to start eating some. If the milk had started to go sour before the rennet was added, especially in hot weather, the cheese was something like Caerphilly cheese. If the milk had not turned sour, it would be more like mature cheddar, but tastier. It was lovely to put on a fork and toast in front of the fire.

A butter worker.

A Gower style hedge.

Hedge Laying in Gower
by Trevor Hughes

All the farmers used to do their own hedge laying, and when I was about 15, I laid my first hedge. I was quite pleased with it, until a farmer riding past in his pony and trap said, "Who taught you to lay a hedge, boy?" That made me think! What was wrong with my hedge? I decided to go to the next ploughing and hedging competition to find out how it should be done. I realised that my hedge was cut too high, and eventually the sheep would have been able to scramble through it. From then on I learnt to do it properly, in the Gower style of hedging.

The first task is to clear away the surrounding undergrowth on both sides of the hedge, so that the existing structure is exposed. Then two rows of clots are placed to repair the top of the bank before pleaching can begin. Pleachers are cut stems – cut and laid at angle of 45% and then crook stakes are used to hold the cut stems. In the Gower style of hedge laying, a double row of crook stakes is used, placed alternately on either side of the centre of the hedge. Eventually, a new hedge will grow from the established roots, and in the meantime, the laid pleachers act as a living barrier.

Nowadays, hedge laying is a specialised skill, but hedge-laying competitions still take place in Gower. This is the judge's method of scoring –

Effectiveness against stock	30 marks
Choice of pleachers and their angle	15 marks
Heel cleanliness, length and low cut, absence of bark damage	25 marks
Ditch	10 marks
Finish – including staking and firmness	20 marks
Total	100 marks.

THE SHEPHERD FAMILY, STAVEL HAGAR (BUTCHERS AND SMALLHOLDERS)
by Beryl Dunn

Four generations of the Shepherd family – Frank, Beryl, Stephen and Richie.

My grandfather Frank Shepherd married Margaret Dix, Stavel Hagar. They lived at first in Willow Cottage, and later moved to Stavel Hagar, where my grandfather had a smallholding. He kept horses for ploughing, and spent hours polishing his horse brasses and the leather bridles. The horses would be brushed until they were gleaming, and their manes would be combed and plaited. They would be quite a sight going through the village. My grandfather was the same with his tools – I can see him now, every spade and hoe had to be cleaned and oiled. He was very meticulous!

My father Richie Shepherd worked alongside him, and they chatted together all day long. They always got on well. They grew watercress in the beds in Stavel Hagar, and a variety of vegetables for market.

When I left school, my father bought a milk round. We had eight cows and it was my job to milk them. We would turn them out on The Groose to graze. My sister Peggy went out one evening to get them in. My father went to see what was taking her so long – and found that she was trying to bring in someone else's cows! I would be up at 6.30 a.m. milking, and then the milk was put into a cooler. Later it would be put into containers and my father and I would set off on our round. It took us to Penclawdd, Crofty and Llanmorlais – we would cross the line at the station to deliver to the houses on the other side.

My father was also a butcher, and would help Ambrose Austin, Newton Farm, if there were bullocks to be slaughtered. He would slaughter sheep and pigs at Stavel Hagar. I remember sitting on the stairs of the slaughterhouse watching him. We thought nothing of it – we were used to it! My father had a van and would drive around Gower selling his meat, and every Saturday he went with my mother to Swansea Market where he had a stall.

I remember one occasion when my father was badly bitten by a pig.

Dora Jones . . .
That was our pig! We spoiled him, and found it hard to take him to the butcher. We had to walk him down the Stavel Hagar at 9 o'clock in the morning. On the way down, the gate of Big House was open, and he trotted in there. He went inside and was standing by the grate. We got him out eventually, and left him in Stavel Hagar. The animals weren't slaughtered straight away – they had to cool off. I went home, and at about 1 o'clock I heard him squealing. That always upset me! Afterwards there was a lot of work to do salting the meat.

The Day We Killed The Pig
Remembered by Janie Hutin

Bacon was the main meat for most farmers in my youth – they would keep a sow and breed their own pigs for selling, and also would keep some for their own use. It was not only farmers who had pigs – a familiar sight in most villagers' gardens was a poultry shed, and a pig sty. The villagers would produce their own vegetables, bacon and eggs.

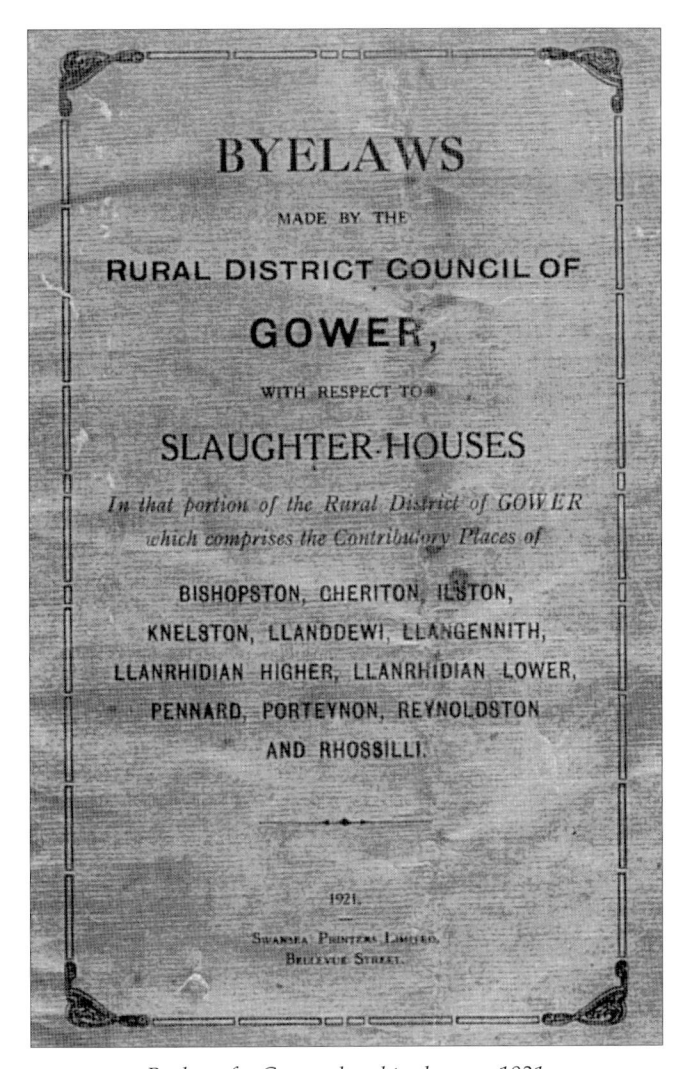

Byelaws for Gower slaughter houses, 1921.

When the pig was ready for killing, it was a busy time for everyone. Most farms had an outside boiler, and before the butcher arrived, plenty of wood would have been chopped, so that there would be a good supply of boiling water.

The butcher would arrive and the pig would be laid on a bench, where the butcher would cut its throat with a long sharp knife. (Later they were stunned before being killed.) Once the pig was dead, all the hair would be scalded with boiling water, and scraped off with 'candlesticks' – metal instruments, shaped like candlesticks, which the butcher brought with him. Once the pig was clear of its hair, it would be taken into a room to be hung up. We took our pig to the back kitchen where it would be hung by its back legs from the beams. The butcher would cut it down the middle, and take out all the stomach. The covering over the intestines (called the scarf) would be taken off, washed and kept for faggots. The heart and the liver would be saved, and the bladder given to boys for a football.

Probably the next day, the butcher would return to cut up the pig. First the head would be cut off, then the backbone (called the chine), leaving the two sides. The ham would be cut off each side, and most of the ribs and slices of steak, leaving a flat smooth surface. Now came the work for the women. The sides and hams would be placed on the slab in the dairy – our slab had raised sides, the space in the middle would hold the salt and the brine. Blocks of salt would be cut up and mixed with salt petre, and then a layer of the mixture was put onto the slab, and also rubbed well into meat. It would stay there for a few weeks so that the meat would be well preserved for the rest of the year.

The head would be trimmed, cut up and boiled to make brawn. The liver was minced with onions, breadcrumbs, sage, salt and pepper. The scarf would be cut up big enough to hold a few spoonfuls of the mixture, and the faggots would be put into tins and cooked in the oven.

The meat would also be shared with our neighbours and friends. The hams and bacon would be taken from the brine and hung up from hooks in the beams in the kitchen until it was dry – the hams would be stored in muslin.

Fresh meat would only be bought on a Saturday for Sunday dinner.

Nancy Payne, née Dunn, remembers . . .
My grandfather Richard Jenkins farmed at Pengwern Farm, Llanrhidian. We lived with him there and would kill four pigs between January and April. Bacon was our staple diet – we would have bacon for breakfast, boiled bacon and vegetables for dinner and our supper would be cold bacon and pickles. Whenever we cooked the bacon we would have bowls of dripping – the rashers mostly consisted of fat with a little lean meat – and on this supposedly 'unhealthy' diet, most of my family lived into their 90s.

Nothing was wasted, the day we killed the pig. My grandmother would catch the blood from the pig when it was hot, and put it in a bowl in the well to congeal it. It would then be mixed with sage, onion, thyme and breadcrumbs. The pig's liver would be used for faggots, and we would have spare ribs and pork steaks. The meat obtained from around the pig's neck we called 'broken meat'. This would be stored in a big stone jar – one layer of salt, and one layer of meat and would be boiled with vegetables in the winter. We would boil the pig's head to obtain brawn, and even the trotters would provide a meal. The meat would then last us all year round.

The Meat Round
by Audrey Williams

My grandmother, Mrs. Annie Austin of Newton, had a butchers business – this entailed not only taking the meat to Swansea Market on Saturdays, but also a local delivery of meat to the villagers every Friday afternoon.

When my uncle Ambrose was well and able to do this, the trap would be loaded up with the meat wrapped in snowy white cloths and placed in large baths or baskets. Off he would go with Simon his faithful horse pulling the trap. The trap was enclosed with a canvas-like covering to help keep out the rain or sometimes the snow. The first call would be to the houses opposite the school – Highbury and Glenroy – then on to Oldwalls and to Leason. His last port of call was always the Mill, having called in most of the houses on the way down through the village.

In the Mill there was always a lovely fire waiting for him, and a welcome cup of tea – probably supper too! Later the cards would come out and he would join Mr. and Mrs. Thomas John Willis, Stanley and Dulcie in a game of whist. Now on one particular Friday night, Simon came home on his own, pulling the empty trap. Can you imagine the concern this caused Maisie, Ambrose's wife, and his mother? I think it was my mother Annie who ran all the way to the Mill – no telephones in those days – and found Ambrose still playing cards, quite happily beside the fire. He had forgotten the time, but poor old Simon had had enough and had decided to come home and have his supper and a lie down in the stable. I think this was the only time this happened; probably he had such a telling off from the womenfolk that he didn't risk having that last game of cards again.

After Ambrose died of TB at the early age of 47, in 1944, my mother Annie continued with the meat round, often getting wet and cold as the covered wagon did not offer much protection. She also had the worry during the war years of food coupons, as meat was rationed. It was difficult for my mother when a customer spotted a nice leg of lamb to explain that they couldn't have it as they didn't have enough coupons.

However, the meat round enabled her to see many of her friends, have a little chat and keep up with the weekly news. This was one of the privileges of village life, to meet and communicate one with another, and to share each other's joys and sometimes sorrows.

Mr. and Mrs. Harry Gordon.
(Photograph provided by Mel Clare).

HARRY GORDON'S SHOP, MALT HALL
Remembered by Janie Hutin

Mr. and Mrs. Harry Gordon kept a shop on the corner of Malt Hall. It sold pop, sweets, tobacco and newspapers. Harry Gordon was also a watch repairer. The shop was joined on to the end of the house, and was a wooden building with a shed below where the younger men of the village played cards and darts. Harry Gordon was a wonderful character! If there was a gale, he would spend all night outside under a hedge, as he was afraid that the roof of his house was going to blow off. His wife would keep him going with cups of tea!

THE OLD POST OFFICE, LLANRHIDIAN
Recalled by Dick Beynon

Although postmen appeared on the 1861 and 1871 census returns, the first Post Office didn't open in Llanrhidian until 1890, when my grandfather William Davies was appointed, and he remained in office for over thirty years.

Miss Lily Davies, later Beynon.

Later, my mother Lily Beynon became post woman, and on special occasions when there would be a heavy mail, she would walk over to Reynoldston to pick up the letters. She would cross Cefn Bryn following the 'postman's path'. This path led from the road by the school, across the fields of Freedown, and over Cefn Bryn to Reynoldston. I remember

The Old Post Office, Llanrhidian.

walking with her one day when a fog came down and we lost our bearings. It was a frightening experience!

My mother's delivery route would take her down through the village, along Coal Lane and past Lane House, up the footpath to Llwyn Derw, on to the Common and Wernhalog, then on to Llanellan and Welsh Moor, returning past the Prisk to the village.

This was her route every day, in all weathers, if there were letters to be delivered to every house.

Mr. & Mrs. Jeffreys, Flora and Victor.

The Shop at Coed-y-Dŵr, Oldwalls
by Janie Hutin

During the 1930s, there was a little shop in Coed-y-Dŵr. The owners were Mr. and Mrs. Robert Jeffreys, Victor and Flora's parents. It was a small wooden building on the side of the front entrance to the house. Coed-y-Dŵr was a small farm, keeping some poultry, and a few cows. Flora used to sell the milk around the village. She rode a bike, with her milk in a can on the handlebars. In the shop were sweets and tobacco products. I don't know when it closed. Victor was a butcher in later years, and had a slaughterhouse behind the house. He used to come to Freedown to kill our pigs.

John Harry, Tailor
by Janie Hutin

Opposite the North Gower Hotel, Mr. and Mrs. John Harry had a shop. John Harry was a tailor and lived in Lane House, at the bottom of the village. He taught his eldest daughter to be a tailoress too. He used to stay up late at night, to finish a funeral order, and Dora used to help him. Everyone had to have a black suit. I remember her telling me how hard it was to sew black clothes with just lamps and candles – no electricity in those days!

The shop also sold sweets, and in the summertime they also sold teas. When the shop closed down, my father bought it, and brought it all in one piece to Freedown Farm, to use as a store shed.

Cross House, Llanrhidian
*Remembered by Hilda Davies,
in conversation in 1980 with Eric Morgan*

The shop belonged to my grandmother, Mary Grove, and she left it to her eldest daughter Beatrice. Beatrice married Willie Winch, Stavel Hagar, who was blind, and he would sell tea around Gower. My brother Ernie was allowed to take Mondays off school so that he could accompany

Beatrice & Willie Winch

Willie on his round. Willie sold many varieties of tea, which he could identify by touch. He was also the church organist.

Many village girls came to work in the shop, including Dorothy Edwards who was there for many years, Nancy Winch and Lottie May, who was an evacuee.

My father would go to Swansea in his horse and trap to buy provisions, but 'we grew our own bacon'. We fed six pigs, and then Tom Tucker would come to kill them. I always dreaded that time! I also used to sell ice-cream, and the ice would arrive from Swansea on the bus.

GEORGE AND RACHEL DAVIES AT THE DOLPHIN
Remembered by Gwennie Winch, née Davies

George and Rachel Davies in the garden of The Dolphin.

My father George Davies was called 'George the Mill' because his father had built Higher Mill House, and George was born the night the family moved in.

Like his father before him, George became licensee of the Dolphin Inn, Llanrhidian, which was then owned by Buckley's Breweries. (The villagers remember that the pub in those days had sand on the floors

The Concert Party, 1935.
Gwennie Davies with Peggy Kent, Nancy Jeffreys, Brenda Jones, Hilda Kent, Ivy Thomas, Emily Williams, Nancy Winch, Hazel Kent, Marjorie Williams, and Mavis Williams.

The Dolphin Inn, May 1937, decorated for the Coronation celebrations.

and a spittoon in the bar.) Thomas Gordon of The Hollies and Frank Harry of Berwick Cottage were regular customers at The Dolphin, and with George as 'Prime Minister' were known as 'The Cabinet'.

George's sister Polly and her husband Harry lived in Lower Mill Cottage and brought up seven children there.

When I was very young and my grandfather was licensee, I remember a drayman saying that I had saved his life. When he was in the trenches in France during World War I, he was woken up by the sound of my voice calling, "Macca! Macca!" – my pet name for him. He jumped out of the trench, which was immediately shelled.

At the age of 15, I went into service in London for the family of Sir John Llewellyn, Penllergaer, but returned home to Llanrhidian when my young sister Muriel died.

I used to organise Shrove Tuesday concerts for the young girls in the village, which would be held in the church hall to packed audiences.

Although I am now 93 years old, and left Llanrhidian in 1947, whenever I talk about Llanrhidian, I call it 'down home'.

Lil Long at the Dolphin
by John Long

My father was a professional golfer, but unfortunately he contracted tuberculosis meningitis, so planning ahead, he and my mother took over the Dolphin Inn in March 1945. Dad was the Licensee. He died in September leaving our mother Lil to run the pub with us three small children.

Nellie Davies and Mrs. Lil Long outside the Dolphin.

The Dolphin was a Hancocks Brewery pub and when Dad died, we were given notice to quit. Luckily, on hearing this, the villagers got together and told the Brewery that if they got rid of Mrs. Long and her children then they would boycott the pub forever. The Brewery gave my mother six months trial to see if she could cope with running the pub on her own, and she ended up staying there for 21 years.

That shows the friendship and camaraderie of the villagers and I will always be grateful to them for this act of kindness.

Mrs. Long and Brian behind the Dolphin Bar.

A move to the country by Brian Long . . .
It was in March 1945 that we – Mum, Dad, Pat, John and myself – moved from Fforestfach to the Dolphin Inn in Llanrhidian. My father, Tom, had some experience of running a bar, and with the support of my mother they had high hopes of making a success of the venture. Sadly, our father died within six months and so Mum had to take on the mammoth job herself.

The conditions were fairly primitive in as much as there was no running water in the pub and consequently no water toilets neither for our customers or us. These amenities we had taken for granted in our previous home, so it was a bit of an experience to say the least to have to bath in front of the fire every Sunday in a zinc bath. It was even more of an experience to have to empty the toilet whenever it was required. John and I used to go down to the open water pipe at the side of the river each morning, to fill a milk churn with the clear fresh water, and take it back to Mother so that she would have a supply for the needs of the pub

John, Pat, Mrs Lil Long and Brian.

and the kitchen for the day. This would be repeated if needed, when we returned from school.

We each had our chores to do, mostly at weekends. Pat always helped with the cleaning, and John and I helped with re-stocking the bar and cellar, washing the back and paths down with rain water that had been collected in a large water tank. Each evening, we three kids used to sit in the parlour doing homework, reading or listening to the radio. The light switches for the pub were all in the parlour and we had had a system whereby at Mother's request someone in the bar would knock the connecting door. One knock meant put the bar light on; two knocks and we would put the dartboard light on – and the dreaded three knocks meant that the toilet needed emptying, so it was out with the torch, the shovel (and the clothes pegs), and up the garden path John and I would go to 'dig for victory', to the chorus of "Good boys, don't be long, we're bursting!" Whilst John and I were doing our bit, Pat was cutting up squares of paper to hang in the toilet (no shiny magazine paper allowed).

At a set time each evening, we'd wend our way through the bar to go upstairs to bed – the staircase was between the bar and the smoke room – and then Mother would lock the door again after us for security. Later when the Brewery was forced on health grounds to modernise the Dolphin, we had a bathroom, hot and cold running water, and the pub had its own toilets with brass fittings that we would have to polish every day.

I never look back and think of any our past experiences with regret. We all loved the village, the people and the friendships we made and are still making. Even though John and I don't live in the village, a part of us is always there. Pat, of course, is where she's always wanted to be – home!

WILL HARRY, CILLIBION FARM
Remembered by his niece, Marjorie Williams

Uncle Willie was my mother's brother, and lived in Cillibion Farmhouse. In 1906, his father bought him his own traction engine, and he went to the Fowler works in Leeds, to meet the team that were going to build it. He stayed on at the factory as the engine was being assembled, and in December 1907 the completed engine arrived at Gowerton station. He named it 'Dauntless'.

Willie used the engine to power threshing machines, and also for haulage. He also went to Carmarthen where he used the Dauntless to power portable rack saws to cut timber.

Willie married Annie Beynon of Llethrid and they moved to Lunnon, but Annie was homesick for Llethrid and they returned to live in the Lodge there.

Willie went on to buy a total of sixteen steam traction engines.

The Dauntless, hauling hay to the hay merchants in Swansea, 1912.

Sawing in Carmarthenshire, 1920.

5

Leisure Time

> GLAMORGANSHIRE.
> ## LLANRHIDIAN FAIRS,
> *(TOLL FREE)*
> WILL be held annually at the village of Llanrhidian, the 22d of February, Palm-Monday, and the 3d of October, for the sale of Cattle, Horses, Sheep, &c. The day following each of those days a Fair will be held for the sale of Pigs.
> N. B. Shoemakers, Hatters, Hawkers, &c. will find here a ready sale for their goods.
> Llanrhidian village lies eleven miles west of Swansea, to which place there is a good road.

Notice for Llanrhidian Fair.

Wilma Collins recalls . . .
My grandmother Mary Grove lived in Cross House, and would always make sure that the water butt seen here in the painting was filled the day before the fair. The fair would take place on the green outside the

Cross House.

church. My grandmother would then make penny and ha'penny buns to sell at the fair. This would have been before the First World War.

The Oddfellows' Lodge, Llanrhidian

*Oddfellows in procession past the Welcome to Town.
Richard Dunn, Little Cillibion, is in this photograph, which was probably taken by his son Willie.*

In the *Cambrian* newspaper on the 26th April 1867, it is recorded that a dispensation was granted to open a new lodge at Llanrhidian, Gower, in the house of Mr. Thomas Davies, Dolphin Inn, the lodge to be called the Rock of Friendship. Later, the lodge room was moved to the Welcome to Town, and every year the Oddfellows would alternately walk to the church or chapel to hold a service there.

Mr. Glyn Grove, Llwyn Derw was the Secretary of the Lodge for over fifty years.

Ernie Grove received a gift of cigarettes from the Oddfellows when he was a prisoner-of-war in Germany, and remembers that you would receive a bounty if you took a fox's tail to a meeting.

> ODDFELLOWS' DEMONSTRATION AT LLANRHIDIAN.
> —On Friday last the Rock of Friendship Lodge of the Manchester Unity held its anniversary. The Brethren mustered at their Lodge-room in the morning (joined by the District Officers and friends from Swansea, who had gone down to take part in the proceedings), and headed by a brass band, formed in procession, and marched to the Old Walls Chapel, where an excellent sermon was delivered by the worthy minister of the place. On leaving the place of worship, the Brethren proceeded to Fairy Hill, the seat of Starling Benson, Esq., where they met with a hearty reception. From thence they marched on to Stouthall, returning by way of Cefn Bryn. Arrived back, the Brethren sat down to a substantial dinner, provided by the host and hostess of the Dolphin, to which the party did ample justice, they having journeyed over several miles of country, and were well prepared for the repast. This promising little lodge numbers 42 members, and is in a thriving condition

Oddfellows Demonstration at Llanrhidian, 1867.

Llanrhidian Rugby Team.
Capt. Glyn Grove holding rugby ball, also included are George and Jack Thomas, Albert Williams, John Hopkins, Ivor Parry, Dick Dunn, Austin Grove and Bert Dunn.

Sport in Llanrhidian

Kenny Williams recalled the sports that were played in Llanrhidian – there were tennis courts behind the forge in Oldwalls, and a cricket and football pitch in George Thomas's field opposite the Greyhound. The footballers played in a league, and George Thomas would take them to matches in his charabanc. Kenny Williams adds that the "old village boys always played rugby."

Llanrhidian Quoits Team
Remembered by Ernie Grove

We had a wonderful quoits team in the village – they won the Gower League Cup. The games would be played on weekends, and then they would all troop to the pub – win or lose! The pubs would do a roaring trade, not only with the quoiters but also with trippers who would

Llanrhidian Quoits Team, in the 1930s.
Bert Morris, Stan Gordon, Basil Williams, Ashley Pearce, Stan Jones, Tom Harris, Jack Jones, Gower Davies, Leslie Williams, Will Grove, Will Thomas, Lenny Williams, Haydn Williams, Kenny Williams, Brynley Grove, Victor Jeffreys and Richard Williams.

In the foreground is the Quoits Pitch.

arrive in charabancs from town to watch the matches. We had a good quoits bed, with the bank behind where everyone sat. The hill was clear then as there were always sheep to nibble away at the brambles and bushes. When we were lads we used to slide down the hill from top to bottom on our heels, dodging the bushes. The quoits bed was on the old mill pond near the church. It was covered in a layer of clay. I once went with Ashley Pearce and his horse and cart to fetch some clay. We brought it from Cwm Cynor Lane in Crofty.

A log of wood was placed in the centre of the bed, and then the clay was laid down and levelled off. It reached almost to the top of the upright log, which had an iron peg in it. Then they would put a feather or piece of paper on the peg. Kenny Williams was an expert at laying the quoit bed and then he acted as umpire, using callipers to measure the distances. Strong wood was used to surround the bed; it needed to be tough, as the quoits would fly into it.

They had some good players in the team. My brother Brynley was one, and Victor Jeffreys the butcher was the other. They scored by how many quoits they got near the peg – up to 21 – I think that was the way it was, if I remember rightly. I don't know how it faded out because it was very popular. It was a pity to see it go. I used to practice on the quoit bed. I would be 'catching on' as they say, not playing the full length, but I would hit my knee with the quoit. Painful it was! A bit too young I was, and not strong enough.

The Church Hall

The church hall was the social centre of the village. It was the meeting place for the Mothers' Union and WI, and harvest suppers, whist drives and dances were held there. Every year plays were enacted by church and chapel members to full houses.

When the new school was opened in 1910, Kenny Williams recalled that the hall was used as a Men's Institute, where newspapers were delivered every day. One side of the partition was the reading room and library, and the other side was the games room, where dominoes, draughts and cards were played. He recalled: "I have seen two men playing draughts, and not finish it the same night. They would go back the next day. Cyril Jeffreys was a good draughts player as was Tom Harry. Very keen! The younger members had to leave at 9 p.m. – once 9 o'clock came, out they had to go!"

Whist Drives

Whist drives were very popular in the church hall – especially the Christmas Whist Drive when the first prize would be a turkey, the second a goose, and third prize was a chicken. There would be so many people attending these evenings that extra tables would have to be put out on the stage.

Llanrhidian's Mothers' Union
by Beryl Dunn

*Rev. and Mrs. J. Davies.
Under Mrs. Davies's leadership, the membership
of the Mothers' Union increased.*
(Photograph provided by Mrs. Ivy Griffiths).

Llanrhidian Mothers' Union celebrated its 90th anniversary in January 2004. The branch was formed on the 8th January 1914, when a meeting was held in the parish room, at which Lady Lyons of Kilvrough was present, together with the diocesan president Mrs. Kate Puxley, who was the guest speaker. The attendance was rather disappointing, but under the leadership of Mrs. Davies, the vicar's wife, numbers rose steadily, and the branch has flourished ever since.

Over the years a varied programme of speakers and events have been held and members have regularly attended deanery and diocesan events. To mark this milestone event, the 90th anniversary was celebrated by a luncheon attended by members and guests.

THE EARLY YEARS OF LLANRHIDIAN WOMEN'S INSTITUTE

*Remembered by Violet Morgan,
in conversation with Eric Morgan, 1986*

*Llanrhidian's Women's Institute.
Back row –Ellen Sparkes, Dorothy Williams. 2nd row – Flora Jeffreys. 3rd row – Noreen Gordon, Gladys Williams, Maisie Austin, May Crocker, Dora Jones, Lucretia Pritchard, Peggy Shepherd, Marjorie Williams, Front row – Mary O'Keefe, Violet Morgan, Louisa Davies, Alice O' Keefe and Louisa Jeffreys.*

Violet Morgan was a founder member of Llanrhidian Women's Institute, attending the first meeting arranged by Mrs. J. Davies, the vicar's wife, and Mrs. J. Morgan, the minister's wife, in 1919. Ruth Gordon was the first secretary. It was one of the first branches in the United Kingdom, and the third oldest in the Glamorgan Federation of W.I.s. In 1921, Violet Morgan was appointed secretary for two years, and later was the secretary for sixteen years. She was also elected president four times, including during the group's Golden Jubilee in 1969.

"When we started," recalled Violet, "the membership fee was one shilling and we had more than seventy members, including five or six men. We met every week for thirty years; the members would all walk to the meetings that were held by the light of oil lamps in the village hall. Demonstrators, like the two Misses Hill from Horton, would teach us new skills like raffia work, sea-grass stools, tatting and eiderdown making. I would use the feathers from our Christmas geese. We would also have thrums delivered from a carpet factory, so that we could make rugs. The Misses Hill would also give talks about their travels in India."

When the group moved to the new school, the rooms were still lit by lamps until the arrival of electricity in the 1930s. By this time, the fee was six shillings and six pence a night, and the group would hold many fundraising events, such as whist drives or dances, where The Bandits from Gowerton would provide the music. They also held raffles – one prize was a rug, knitted by members that had won first prize in the Gower Show.

Violet remembered that, "We had to have permits during the war years to get sugar for jam making, and we also were allowed a small ration for our meetings. During these years, we did a lot of knitting for the forces – all in khaki or air force blue wool. We also knitted clothes for the children of liberated countries after the war. In addition we entered many shows – exhibiting produce and handicrafts."

The W.I. in Llanrhidian has continued to meet without a break since 1919.

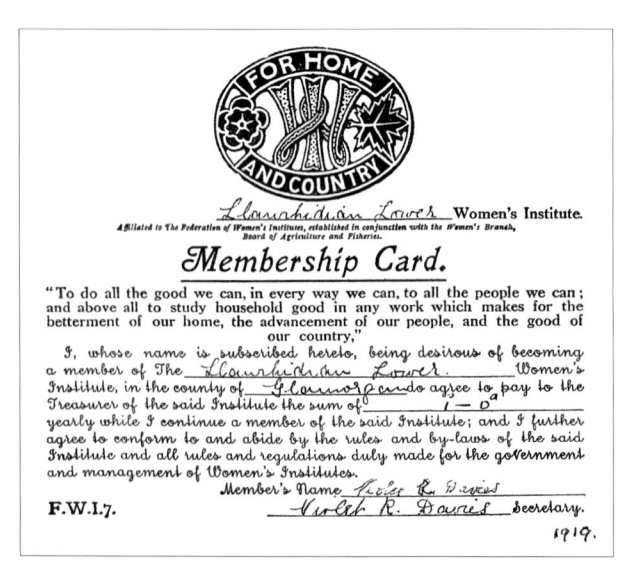

LEISURE TIME

The Bachelors' Supper.
Every year, the bachelors of the village served a supper to the villagers in the church hall.
Included here are: Glyn Thomas, Victor Jeffreys, Will Hopkins, Marion Thomas, May Bevan, Sally Bevan, Glyn Mabbett, Eric Shepherd, Mary O'Keefe, Lottie George, Dai Jones The Prisk, Cyril Jeffreys, Ronald Winch, Dick Beynon, Doris Gordon, Cliff Jenkins, Tom Harry, Albert and Ivor Thomas, Leonard Jones, John Williams, Stan Gordon, Glyn Clement, Nancy Winch and Mrs. Winch.

The Bandits.

VILLAGE DANCES
Remembered by Dulcie Olstersdorf

The village dances took place every Saturday evening in the church hall. The dances began at 7.30 p.m. until 10.30 p.m. when the last bus left the Cross. The dances were very popular, and the hall would be packed with young people travelling from the Gower villages to enjoy themselves and meet their friends there. Christie Tucker and Sid Williams would be at the door taking the admission money, and if you went outside, you had to get your hand stamped; otherwise you would have to pay again to get in. The music was provided by a band – there was The Bandits (the three Williams sisters – Ida who played the piano, Joan on the violin and Nora on the ukulele banjo. Harold Williams, who married Ida, was on the drums). Ron Parry and his band also played, as did Ossie Vaughan and his accordion band from Gowerton, and Jenkins from Bishopston.

At the end of the evening, the last bus would be packed so tightly, that there were people on every stair, and the platform could be heard dragging on the ground!

New Year's Eve Dance
The highlight of the year was the New Year's Eve Dance organised by Mrs.

Beynon, Penrhallt, to raise funds for the District Nurses in Reynoldston. She would provide soft drinks and delicious cakes. The hall would be full until just before midnight when everyone would go outside to hear the bells of Llanelli ring in the New Year.

OLDWALLS YOUNG PEOPLE'S GUILD
by Janie Hutin

'The Happiest Days of Your Life', February 1955.
Back row – George Richards, Betty Clement, Donald Lewis, Beryl Hughes, William John Davies, Pearl Roberts, Glyn Rogers and Edna Jenkins.
Front row – Yvonne Jenkins, Rev. Medford Lloyd, Cynthia Jones, David Gordon and John Hutin.

In 1950, Rev. Medford Lloyd came to the pastorate of the chapels of Oldwalls, Burry Green, Cheriton and Llangennith. He and his wife Gwladys and their two sons stayed in Gower for six years, living in the Manse at Burry Green – no electricity, no sewage, and no piped water. Rev. Medford Lloyd travelled around Gower on his motorbike. He not only had the Sunday services, Sunday school and Rota services which needed long distances to travel, he had weeknight meetings, Young People's Guild and Band of Hope as well as visiting the sick. A very busy life!

The Band of Hope meetings, lasting about an hour, started with a hymn and a prayer, then all sorts of activities were held. Sometimes a speaker would attend. All the meetings in Oldwalls were held in the Vestry. The Young People's Guild would meet every Friday night, and every year a play would be performed. Rev. Medford Lloyd was very 'do-it-yourself' minded and was capable of taking on any job. He decided that plays could not be performed without scenery, and the only way to have some was to make our own. The boys had the job of making the structure from wooden battens, which were made by sawing up scrap timber and nailing them together to form 'flats' which we covered with old lino and cardboard. The girls' job was to paste wallpaper over the flats that were repapered every year. A few flats would have spaces cut out for a door and window. We also made our own lighting. Mr. Lloyd used his children's empty tins of National Dried Milk painted black and cut to make the backing for the bulbs, with sheets of coloured plastic to put in front – those were our footlights! He made a wonderful switchboard, which had ordinary and silent switches, dimmers for night time, bells for the telephone, door rings and spotlights. It was a very busy time before we started learning our lines!

We started in 1952 with 3 one-act plays, so that we could get accustomed to performing on stage. As members of the Guild came from Llangennith and Llanmadoc as well as Llanrhidian, it was decided that the plays would be performed in each village hall. Our first performance took place in April. A full dress rehearsal was held in Llanrhidian church hall before the first night, then the second and third would be performed in Llanmadoc and Llangennith church halls. Of course, it was not just the performances on the night, the scenery had to be taken down and taken to each hall to be put up before the night. As most of the members were either in school or working, it was the ones living on the farms who moved the scenery, we could take time off!

The Happiest Days of Your Life

CHARACTERS
(in order of their appearance)

Dick Tassell (Assistant Master at Hilary Hall)	Donald Lewis
Rainbow (School Porter and Groundsman) ...	John Hutin
Rupert Billings (Senior Assistant Master at Hilary Hall)	Wm. John Davies
Godfrey Pond (Headmaster of Hilary Hall) ...	Medford Lloyd
Miss Evelyn Whitchurch (Principal of St. Swithin's School for Girls)	Cynthia Jones
Miss Gossage (Senior Assistant Mistress of St. Swithin's)	Pearl Roberts
Hopcraft Minor (Pupil at Hilary Hall)	David Gordon
Barbara Cahoun (Pupil at St. Swithin's) ...	Yvonne Jenkins
Joyce Harper (Assistant Mistress at St. Swithin's)	Beryl Hughes
The Rev. Edward Peck	George Richards
Mrs. Peck (His Wife)	Betty Clement
Edgar Sawter	Glyn Rogers
Mrs. Sawter (His Wife)	Edna Jenkins

Stage Manager: Edward Rees
Stage Hands, etc.: Lynn Pritchard, Victor Richards
Dressers and Make-up, etc.: Janie Clement, Audrey John

Programme, 'The Happiest Days of Your Life', 1955.

It would take most of the morning to fix everything for the night, and it was always a great relief when the lights worked for the first time. The late Gethin John, Tyrcoed, moved everything on his tractor and trailer. As we were performing three plays, the scenery had to be changed, so we had a singer to perform between each play.

In 1953, Mr. Lloyd decided that we were experienced enough to perform a 3-act play, which was much easier on the scenery. We had got 'modernised' by now. Donald Lewis would drive his father's lorry and move the scenery to the halls much more quickly. By now the plays had become very popular, so we decided to hold three performances in Llanrhidian hall. Now the audience could come to us! The hall was full every night, with boys even sitting on the window sills. No fire restrictions in those days!

In 1956, the Rev. Medford Lloyd left us for Newport, and the Rev. Tudor Lloyd came to the pastorate. The Guild continued to produce plays for a few more years, but sadly television had become popular, cars were more plentiful and most of us had family commitments so the Guild as we knew it came to an end.

It had been a very happy time. We had all enjoyed taking part in the various plays even with rumbling stomachs and forgotten lines. Our prompters kept us going!

Llanrhidian Carnivals

Both church and chapel held carnivals in the summer, the church in a field at Penrhallt, and the chapel in a field at Freedown Farm.

The Church Carnival
remembered by Marjorie Williams . . .

A dance would be held in the Church hall to choose the Carnival Queen, and on the day of the carnival, everyone would meet at the Cross. The Carnival Queen and her attendants would ride on the back of George Thomas's lorry, while the rest of the villagers, mostly in fancy dress, would walk in procession from the Cross to the carnival field at Penrhallt.

Summer Carnivals at Freedown Farm
remembered by Janie Hutin . . .

The carnival was an annual event at Freedown Farm. It was held in the second field from the road. My father would cut the grass and thistles

The Comic Band, led by Will Morgan played at many village carnivals.

LEISURE TIME

Llanrhidian Carnival, 5th August 1924.
Bessie Clement, Dick Clement and Winnie Williams on 'The Last Load'.

Early 1920s carnival. Mary Gordon and Nancy Dunn.

A 1937 Coronation Celebration with Mavis Williams, Marjorie Williams, Peggy Shepherd and Thelma Williams in the pushchair.

before the carnival day. The boiler would be placed next to Coed-y-Dŵr hedge for safety. There, all the water was heated for the tea that was held in a marquee at the top of the long field. There were the usual stalls – Hoopla, Guess the weight of a sheep, Bric-a-brac stall, and Ratti's ice-cream. One of the main attractions was the skittle alley. Sheepdog trials were held at the bottom of the field – competitors came from miles around, under the watchful eye of Mr. Llewellyn Gordon. The sheep would be kept near the farmhouse, and when the competition was over they would be put through a gap in the hedge into Coed-y-Dŵr field. There was a great deal of work to organise everything, and everyone hoped for a sunny day. It seemed always to have been a great success. Unfortunately, when the 1939-45 war broke out, it all came to an end.

An excursion in a horse brake.
(A photograph from an album of the Shepherd family, Llanrhidian).

Sunday School Trips

Kenny Williams recalled that when he was young, they would travel as far as Mumbles in horse brakes for their Sunday School outing. He remembered that while waiting on the Cross for the brakes to arrive, the boys would put their ears to the ground, listening for the sound of the approaching horses!

Pockett's Bristol Channel Steam Packet Co., Ltd.

Daily Pleasure Sailings

By the Magnificent Saloon
PASSENGER STEAMSHIPS

'Brighton' & 'Mavis'

From Swansea and Mumbles

To Ilfracombe, Clovelly, Lynmouth,
Lundy Island, Tenby, etc., etc.

FOR FARES SEE BILLS.

Further Information can be obtained from :—
POCKETT'S OFFICE, South Dock, Swansea; Pier, Ilfracombe; or
11, Narrow Quay, Bristol.

Ilfracombe was a favourite destination for Church and Chapel Sunday Schools. 1911 advertisement.

1926 outing to Barry Island. Violet Morgan and her son Ronald are in front of the bus.

Ebenezer Chapel Sunday School Trips 1926-39
by Audrey Williams

What wonderful memories these words evoke! All the children of the Sunday School would await this exciting day eagerly. The trips were usually held in June, around about the longest day, so that meant a day off from school, which was an added bonus. The destination of these trips varied each year, for example Weston-super-Mare, Barry Island, Porthcawl and Ilfracombe to mention a few.

When we went to Ilfracombe, we travelled by coach to Mumbles and crossed by boat. Some of us would be terribly sick, but that didn't deter us from putting our hands up again when Ilfracombe was proposed. You see, children in those days were not taken around like they are today. There were very few cars about, and not many parents owned them. So you can imagine the thrill of a trip by coach from Llanrhidian Cross. Oh! Bristol Zoo was another favourite place to visit. This was very popular as most children love animals, and the high spot of the day was to have a ride on Rosie the elephant – I mean this literally too, because I remember as a small child looking down from Rosie's back and thinking what a long way it was to the ground!

We were put to bed early the night before the trip, but we were far too excited to sleep. Then at last, morning came, and we would meet all our friends on the Cross. We usually took sandwiches for the trip and some children would start eating theirs before we had travelled very far,

A chapel trip – included in this photograph are Llewellyn Jones, Bessie Clement, Dick Clement, his sister Bessie, Winnie Williams, Thomas John Willis, Elizabeth Willis, Glyn Jeffreys (Oldwalls), Stanley John (Hills, Reynoldston), John Dunn, Haydn Williams and Katie John.

probably because they hadn't been able to eat any breakfast because of the excitement. Once we boarded the bus, the singing would start. Mostly we sang hymns, but also some popular songs of the day. However, we had some lovely times.

We would return home about 9 o'clock having stopped for fish and chips on the way home. Very tired but very happy children!

No trips were held during the war years, but they were resumed again in 1950.

A chapel Sunday School trip to Tenby, 29th July 1926. Will Morgan, Dick Harry, Stanley Jones, Ernie Thomas and Gordon Harry.

LEISURE TIME

Church Sunday School trip. Included here are: George Tucker (Llangennith), Gladys Harry, Tom Tucker, Aubrey Tucker, Christie Tucker, Cyril Jeffreys, Gladys Winch, Arthur Beynon, Kenny and Patty Williams.

Church Sunday School trip.
Front row, left to right: Ronald Jones, Clifford Jones, Frank Jones, Ivy Thomas, Brenda Jones, Ena Winch, Nancy Winch, Iris Pearce, Will Grove, Doris Gordon, Terry Williams, Hazel Kent, Emily Williams, Hilda Kent, Ida Kent, Roy Grey, Peggy Kent, Glenis Grove, Wilma Grove, Lily O'Keefe, Flora Jeffreys, Elsie Grove. Also included: John Jones, Mary Ann Jones, Dorothy Jones, Myra Jones, Alice May Jones, Frank Jones (senior), Olwen Jones, Louisa Winch, Molly Winch, Laura Winch, Dora Jeffreys, Elisa Jones, Annie Grey, Mrs. Harry Gordon, Lillian Lewis and Norman Tucker – driver.

Sunday School Outing.
Included here are – Alberta Gwyn, Jessie Gwyn, Gladys Dunn, Dora Harry, Gower Davies, Wilfred Davies, Lily Davies, Ivy Davies, Arthur Harry and Emrys Dunn.

A Sunday School trip to Weston-super-Mare for Edna Beynon with Michael and Lynne, Iris Pearce with Howard, Audrey Grove and Ray, Ivy Griffiths with Jennifer and Julian, and Daisy Elliot with Phillip and David.

Broad Pool, 1941.
John Grove, Doris Gordon, Cyril Jeffreys, John Williams, Leonard Jones, Wilma Grove, Brenda Jones, Ernie Grove, Dora Beynon, Frank Jones and Phil Grove.

BROAD POOL
by Ernie Grove

I remember one very cold winter when Broad Pool was frozen over. In the evening, all the cars would park around the edge with their lights on, so that people could skate. Douglas Roberts, the son of the owner of the Greyhound had a motorbike and sidecar, and would go onto the frozen ice dragging a rope behind him, and we boys would hang on to the rope and be pulled around the ice.

LLETHRID SWALLET, LLANRHIDIAN
Remembered by John Long

In March 1952, I was playing football outside the Dolphin one Sunday morning, when a car stopped and the driver asked me if I knew of any caves in the area. In the car was a highly professional caver called

*Woolley's Hole, Landimore, with Maurice Clague Taylor,
his sister Marjorie, and John Long.*

Maurice Clague Taylor, together with his elderly mother and two sisters Marjorie and Eileen. I joined them and took them to a small cave out under the woods called 'White Lady's Grave'. From that day onwards I spent every Saturday and Sunday exploring and digging to enlarge passageways in various caves in the area with the Taylors.

A year later when in Llethrid, I could see the river there going underground and re-emerging a few miles down the valley in Parkmill. Because of the minor success that was achieved in the White Lady's Grave with the Taylor family, I decided to see how far I could follow the river underground.

It was quite difficult on first entering the cave because, due to the quantity of water rushing through the small entrance and passageways, there had obviously been a number of roof collapses, leaving it quite dangerous in certain areas. At that time I decided to wait for the warmer weather, when the movement of water would be a lot less.

On my next visit I was amazed to see that not only had the river practically dried up, but on entering the mouth of the cave I found that since my first visit the water had changed course leaving quite an interesting passage way for me to explore. After about 200 yards, the way on seemed to be a bit higher than the river level and this necessitated quite a lot of a climbing and scrambling along many little caverns with stalagmite and stalactite formations everywhere. My torch picked out some brilliant 'bacon-like' flows, and thousands of stalagmites and stalactites of pink, and blue and yellow, in various sizes and thickness (some 10ft long) filled my eyes. I realised that I had found something special. The main cavern itself was huge. I tried to shine my torch across and upwards and I couldn't see the extent of it either way. In my estimation it could take the Guildhall in Swansea within it quite easily. It was truly magnificent and was really the find of a lifetime.

The following day, Maurice and his family came down to see what I had found. I have never seen anyone so excited, because he had been pot-holing for years, and here was a 16-year-old boy giving him the moment he had dreamt about. The Taylors spent a few years photographing and plotting whenever the water levels allowed entry to Llethrid Swallet, and wrote a number of articles about this special find. A few years later, I joined the RAF and shortly afterwards the cave was closed due to a serious accident to a person not used to the dangerous levels and roof falls.

The Grand Cavern is now lost forever.

Llethrid Swallet

Maurice Clague Taylor has kindly given permission for the reproduction of his personal record of Llethrid Swallet, which he describes as 'the best decorated cave in Wales' – including his photographs and comments.

Introduction to Maurice Clague Taylor's personal record.

Maurice is standing in the Great Hall, which extends at least twice as far again, that should give a very faint impression of its vastness.

This is one of the most attractive pictures we have taken. It seems to express perfectly the almost fairylike and 'Alice in Wonderland' quality of these calcite formations. The stalactites on the left are pure white, and then some cream and beige ones, finally a deeper copper colour.

The reddish brown roof from which they hang is heavily encrusted with white deposits. Eileen is resting against large stalagmite bosses.

In this photograph, the huge stalagmite seems to be poised menacingly over Eileen like some fantastic creature of the netherworld.

Stalactites of all shapes and sizes abound: at least three large 'corkscrews' can be seen. A large stalagmite mound can be seen. Small curtains extend up the steeply sloping roof above the rimstone slopes.

The 'pièce de resistance' in Llethrid. We call it 'The Drapes'. This immense curtain with its striped border is – for all its length – less than a quarter inch thick.

Immediately below 'The Drapes' is this huge stalagmite, fourteen feet high, which we have called 'The Tower of Babel'.

Here it is! All of 9 ft. high! And have you ever seen a stalactite that size? And the dark one alongside is scarcely less immense.

6

Llanrhidian Marsh

The marsh has been used by generations of villagers for grazing their animals. Rush was cut to be used as animal bedding and for thatching hayricks. The village men would lay out fishing lines in the pills, and in every home there was a shotgun, and widgeon would be taken for the pot.

Even the turf was taken – sometimes illegally. During the Second World War the marsh was used as a gunnery range.

The parish council minutes record that in 1921, "Mr. Phillip Tanner called attention to the state of the Marsh lane, which had fallen so much out of repair that it was difficult to bring loads of rush that way."

In 1937, a letter from the Gower Rural District's Council Clerk called attention to those concerned to the "illegality of removing turf from Llanrhidian lower marsh."

The minutes of 1941, record that 'complaints have been received from a number of Commoners that the barbed wire entanglements on Llanrhidian marshes were a real source of danger to the animals grazing there.

Ernie Grove recalls . . .
We all had guns in those days, and we would go out shooting widgeon. My brother was shot in the face by wildfowlers, and Ashley Pearce brought in the body of a man who had been shot dead on the marsh. He took the body to our barn next to the house.

I would go out fishing on Saturdays – my day off. First, I would bait the lines with lug, and then I would go back two hours after a high tide to pick up the fish. Any later, and they would have been taken by gulls! I usually caught sea bass and flats. It didn't matter if it was dark – I would use the lights of Pwll, Llanelli, as a guide.

In summer, on a Saturday, we youngsters would ride on our bikes to Wernhalog, leaving them on the bank there. We would walk out onto the marsh until we reached the pill, then we would dive into the water and swim. You could feel the difference between the layers of pill water and sea water. The pill water was much colder, and as you dived in, the water would change from warm to cold.

Will Morgan, who had been in the Royal Navy, was an excellent swimmer, and he would swim and dive. We all liked to watch him – we thought that he was wonderful!

Jeff Griffiths . . .
Many of the old cottages in Llanrhidian had rights to cut rush on the marsh, and the flat easily cut areas would be soon claimed. Men would often drive stakes into the ground to deter others from their patch. However, if the horses used to gather the rush were not marsh ponies, and accustomed to crossing the deep pills – marsh ponies never jump a pill – they would become nervous and often damage the shafts of the carts as they tried to jump across, so it suited many farmers to leave the rush cutting to men with experienced horses like my grandfather G. I. Thomas. He would then haul the rush around local farms to be used for animal bedding and thatching the ricks.

Roy Grey . . .
I would help my uncle Ashley Pearce cut rush on the marsh, with a pair of horses and a mowing machine with three cornered blades. I would go out with a mare and a big horse rake, and I would rake the rush into rows. Then we would take a mare and gambo – I would be on top loading and Ashley would be pitching. Everyone would be cutting rush on the marsh in those days – the marsh would be clean, you wouldn't see a blade of grass anywhere!

Rustlers
by Brian Long

As kids in the village, we soon adapted to the way of life and no day was long enough for the things we wanted to do. We had to be forced to come in. We'd put snares down for rabbits, go fishing on the marsh, go out at an unearthly hour to pick mushrooms and pinch apples.

With all the stories of wild duck and geese on the marshes, John and I went looking for a chance to catch a duck or goose – a bit naïve I hear you say – but we were only seven and twelve respectively, and above all, Townies!

We never saw any ducks, not on the ground anyway, but we did see some geese grazing who didn't budge an inch when we approached (this we put it down to the fact that we were upwind). We singled one out and pounced on it with our sticks. John went home to fetch a sack and our pushbike, and on his return we crammed the goose into the sack, loaded it onto the bike and took it home.

To say our mother was surprised would be an understatement, but as there was no going back, we helped to pluck it, and Mother cooked it with the warning to us all that as it was wild, it would almost certainly be very salty.

Dinner time came, what a sight and smell! In those days, a chicken was a real treat, and we all tentatively picked at the salty goose which – lo and behold! – was not salty at all, and was soon gone, to make all those years of wartime rationing seem like a distant memory. As soon as we were able to move, we dug the deepest hole we could find and buried all the evidence, but for weeks we were convinced that the police would come knocking because someone might have seen us with the goose, or even noticed that how well fed we looked, all of a sudden.

Mother said, "Thank goodness no one said anything about wild cattle on the marsh or you boys might have brought a 'wild cow' home!"

Llanrhidian Marsh Pony Improvement Society
by Roy Grey

The Pony Catch.
(Photograph by kind permission of Ken Fox).

At one time, Ashley Pearce had around a hundred mares grazing on the marsh. He would inspect them every Sunday morning, riding his cob as far as Whitford. The horses would be used for haulage, farm work and transport. In 1924, the Llanrhidian Marsh Pony Improvement Society was founded to improve the quality of the ponies there. All the members had grazing rights on the marsh. The society was disbanded on the outbreak of World War II, and reformed in 1959.

The marsh is divided into four sectors – Whitford, Landimore and Leason, Llanrhidian up to Wernffrwd, and Tiller to Salthouse Point. Each autumn, all the horses on the marsh are rounded up on a high tide, and placed in the sector pens. The colt foals are removed for selling. Mares and foals are released back onto the marsh remaining in the sector in which they were born, becoming familiar with the ground and tidal conditions there.

Each spring, four stallions are released, one in each sector, and are rotated annually throughout the four sectors. After eight years, the stallions are sold and replaced with fresh bloodstock.

Llanrhidian Marsh and the Pony Catch
Written by John Hutin

John Hutin.

September tides are very high . . . cars stand in the shadows of the Whipping Stones, their owners engrossed in pony talk. The 'catch' and the arrangements finalised, we would invariably listen to the nostalgic 'when my grandfather was a boy': always pony talk, always back in time, like the ponies that melt in the mist now gathering outside. The fire burns brightly, and the amber in the glasses adds a gleam to the eye, and the thrill of the 'catch' leaves a tingling sensation of expectancy.

The operation depends on the tide, and to some extent, the light. The tides are at their highest, and the amount of dry land is limited, so these conditions make it ideal for a catch. In addition, the streams that through time have scarred the marshlands with steep sided watercourses, act as channels through which the tides press landwards, in miniature bores. These continue until they overspill the banks, transforming the marsh into a wonderful calm sea. Nevertheless, this is a treacherous deception, and the ponies know it as well as the men. They also know the various crossings on their particular part of the marsh, and never venture from them.

So, in the half-light of early morning, three groups of men, each with a distinct task, make their way some miles apart, to their allotted station. The outside group include the fleetest of foot. They are the ones who start the herd on the particular direction desired. The middle group's function is to direct the ponies where there is a diversion of ways, further inland. This acts as a human barrier and an element of surprise is essential. The third group ensures that the ponies are left with no alternative when reaching the tarmac roads, but to arrive at the prepared compound in the village.

The middle group lie on the turf with eyes peeping just above the rush and into the marsh mist. Occasionally a sea bird breaks the shrouded silence with a started call, and the rumbling of the incoming tide is ominous. The nerves tingle, and the teeth clench. Faintly in the distance a new sound akin to muffled drumming.

The ponies are moving in a herd. You know, but you cannot see, but it will not be long now. The drumming is louder, a gradual crescendo, and then you see them, visions of the light brigade! The group of men spaced about twenty yards apart, hug the ground, while the herd wheels and comes bearing directly towards them! Still no one moves. Then, instinctively, the men leap to their feet, brandishing their walking sticks, and the leaders of the herd hesitate in their gallop, and swerve towards the distant Tor. What a glorious breathtaking sight, with manes and tails flowing, bays, chestnuts, duns, greys, all seem to merge into Mother Nature's favourite colours. Then with the confidence that the men in the last group waiting near the Tor will put their past experiences once more successfully to the test, we can relax.

The group laugh and joke, cigarettes are lit, while awaiting the men further out, who started the herd moving. Then together we make our way to the formidable stone walled compound which should now be occupied by the ponies. Soon, the appetite whetted by the salt tang in the air will be satisfied, and the pleasures of an early morning cup of tea will be ours.

Once in the compound, the scene could be any Pony Society. The rigid rules, all horse colts must come off the Marsh. The mares, now docile, are looked over. The stallion is taken for his winter quartering by his keeper. All is orderly, except for the fringes, where bucking colts are capering and having their fling, while small boys are having the time of their lives. Dealers trying to make a deal, and the sun barely over the horizon!

7

I Remember . . .

Wilma Collins . . .
I remember my mother waking my brother Will and me one night to hear a nightingale sing. I wasn't very impressed. I thought that the thrush's song was much more beautiful!

On our land at Llwyn Derw is an area called 'The Arles'. The 'arles' can refer to the hiring of a servant, and probably dates back to the time of the hiring fairs. I remember talking to Cuthbert Pugh, who told me that he was the last man in Gower to have been hired in a hiring fair. He came from Hereford, and stayed in Gower for the rest of his life.

Ernie Grove . . .
I remember that George Thomas hauled a log near to where the bus stop on the Cross is today. We called it 'The Stump'. It was used as a seat so that an audience could watch as the boys of the village performed trick riding on their motorcycles. Ashley Pearce used to take the exhaust off his motorbike, so that it would make quite a racket! We used to say, "Look out! Here comes Hellfire Jack!" when we heard him roar by.

My grandfather, James Grove, was a tailor, and would walk all the way to Neath and back to buy his cloth.

Dick Beynon . . .
I remember Bob Cockney who would walk through the village, ringing a bell and shouting the news.

Roy Grey . . .
I remember the stocking salesman who walked around the village carrying stockings on a long pole like a baseball bat shouting "Sannau lân!"

Emrys Dunn . . .
I remember when I was young, my mother sent me to Penrhallt to buy butter for a neighbour, Mrs. Williams, Hillcrest. I bought the butter – a large round pat – and made my way home. I met some friends and

stopped to play and the butter rolled off down the hill. It was covered in dirt and sheep droppings, but I took it home where I was smacked and sent to bed! My mother went off crossly to buy some more, spending her own money to do so! When she returned, she was even more annoyed to find me sitting on the stairs singing merrily. I think I had another smack for that!

Mrs. Mary Dunn, Nancy and Emrys.

I left the village when I was six years old, but returned to spend my summer holidays there. We boys would go down to the mill pond to play, and one day we built a fine raft out of some old oil drums. We then coaxed Daisy Williams of Seaview Cottage to take it for a test sail. The drums had worked loose, and the raft – and Daisy – sank in the mud!

Nancy Payne, née Dunn . . .
I remember Miss Betsy Bradley of Little Bryn Gwyn. She came from a Devonshire family, and took over the free holding there. She was self-sufficient with a cow, a goat and a pig. She made goat's cheese, and used some of the cow's milk to make beautiful Devonshire clotted cream. This involved keeping the cream in an enamel bowl at a certain temperature beside her black range, but she would never divulge this secret.

We would meet her on the Common every Sunday, on our way to chapel. She would walk from her home to the road in her old boots, carrying her best ones under her arm. When she reached the road, she would hide her old boots under a gorse bush, and then we would all walk to chapel.

Roger Jones . . .
I remember the variety of birds I would see when I lived at Cillibion. Curlews, lapwing, mallard and skylarks nested there, as did some nightjars and yellow hammers. The cuckoo was common, and amongst the gorse there were always adders – especially around the walls of Cae Forgan.

Cynthia Austin . . .
I remember my husband William telling me that there had been a sawpit in the lane almost opposite Newton Farm. It was referred to as 'the soppits' and was a deep pit, used for cross cutting timber, with one man working the saw from above, and the other below.

Beryl Dunn . . .
I remember our neighbours in the 1930s. At Christmas time, my friend Laura and I would go carol singing. We would leave Stavel Hagar and call on Marjorie Williams and her parents at Woodlands, then on to visit Gladys Harry and Esther Harry. We always started giggling here, as Laura's brother Harry, and Reggie Morris would be making fun of us out in the lane. Mrs. Rosie Williams, Seaview Cottage would always have us inside to sing, and at Mrs. Beynon's Penrhallt we would be given a shilling. A lot of money in those days! However one house we went to did not give us such a warm welcome. We were interrupted as soon as we started singing and told, "Go away from here! I just bought a wireless yesterday!"

Ivy Griffiths . . .
I remember when my father kept geese for Christmas time, and the flock would be taken out to fatten on the groose (the short rich salt marsh grazing) at the far reaches of the marsh.

I remember on a Sunday evening, local men used to gather by the rocks up on the hill above where Rocklea is today, to talk about the week's work and interesting topics of the day.

Marjorie Williams . . .
I remember my father showing me a well near Leason called 'Stinking Well'. It had a strong smell of sulphur and was supposed to have curative powers.

Thelma Pritchard . . .
I remember the ancient holy well or "butter pool" in the garden of Baytree House, which was the water supply for the house before the mains came to Llanrhidian. My father Kenny rated highly the curative properties of the water, and would conduct visitors down the path to sample it, using a mug he carried in his pocket for the purpose.

Eric Morgan . . .
I remember the sound of the kettle singing on the hearth, and that women always had mottled legs from sitting close to the fire!

I remember that 'boy' and 'maid' were used to address people of any age, and strangers were 'from off' – 'a feller from off!'

Janie Hutin . . .
I remember in the 1940s and early 50s, that in summertime, all the people who lived on the edge of the Bryn, and kept cows, used to put them to graze on the hill – the Jeffreys of Crickton, the Austins of Newton, Alan Gwyn (Stoneyford), Mrs. Annie Williams (Pant Glas), the Shepherds of New Parks, ours at Freedown and Glyn Jeffreys at Llwyn y bwch. The animals would gather together and wander up the hill. Late afternoon was milking time, but don't worry, the 'Frida' girls will fetch them! This was my sister Betty and myself. We would walk up to Arthur's Stone with our dog, and could easily see the cows from there. Often they would be in Reynoldston, and would start for home when they saw us. When they reached our side of the hill, they would separate and branch out towards their own 'homes'.

This all changed when farmers started selling their milk to the Milk Marketing Board, and the cows had to be milked at a regular time. So keeping cows on the Bryn came to an end.

Jeff Griffiths . . .
I remember when my grandfather George Thomas grew beans in The Croft (the field opposite the church where bungalows were later built). He would grow so many that it would take days to pick them all. They would then be put into mawns (tall wicker baskets) and taken to market.

*

I REMEMBER...

We all remember Esther Harry, who lived under the hill in The Laurels, with her numerous cats. Esther was a distinctive character in the village, with her long black dress, hob nailed boots and black hat.

She worked for many families in the village – feathering geese and chickens in Stavel Hagar, and gardening, cleaning and helping in many homes.

At harvest festival time, Esther would make a circlet of snowberries that she had gathered from her hedge, and they would be used to decorate the church lectern. She is also recorded in the Church magazine as supplying flowers for the altar. Marjorie Williams remembers that she did this when the gillyflowers in her garden were in bloom.

In the only photograph of Esther we can find, she can be seen in the distance watching the wedding of Oswald and Ivy Griffiths. This was typical of Esther, not wanting to miss the occasion, but keeping in the background with modest dignity. This is exactly the way that people in Llanrhidian, with great affection, remember her.

Acknowledgements

David Elliot, Anne Gilbert, Cindy Hyde and Pat Williams, the co-ordinators of Llanrhidian Local History Group, wish to thank –

Awards for All Wales who have provided the funds for the printing of this book.

The County Archivist for access to the Llanrhidian school log books, and the minute books of the Gower Guardians. They are held at the West Glamorgan Archive Services.

S.W. E. P.

Richard at the Cambrian Index.

The Golden Furrow, by A. Ellis Davies.

Maurice Clague Taylor for allowing the reproduction of his personal record of Llethrid Swallet.

The Gower Church Magazines.

Wilma Collins for access to her extensive collection of Gower Church magazines, and for her advice and help.

Eddie John, Dinefwr Press, for his professionalism and patience.

And Martin, for his unfailing support.

All photographs are from the family albums of History Group members unless otherwise acknowledged.

The spelling of place names has varied through the years, so we have followed the latest O/S spellings – except for Stavel Hagar and Cae Forgan, which are spelt in the form used by most people in Llanrhidian.